HEIRS TO
SHAKESPEARE

The goals of Boynton/Cook's *Young Adult Literature* series are twofold: to present new perspectives on young adult literature and its importance to the English language arts curriculum and to offer provocative discussions of issues and ideas that transcend the world of the adolescent to encompass universal concerns about the search for identity, security, and a place in life. The contributing authors are leading teachers and scholars who have worked extensively with adolescents and are well read in the genre. Each book is unique in focus and style; together, they are an invaluable resource for anyone who reads, teaches, and/or studies young adult literature.

Titles in the Series

YOUNG ADULT
LITERATURE SERIES

HEIRS TO SHAKESPEARE

Reinventing the Bard in Young Adult Literature

MEGAN LYNN ISAAC

Boynton/Cook Publishers
HEINEMANN
Portsmouth, NH

Boynton/Cook Publishers, Inc.
A subsidiary of Reed Elsevier Inc.
361 Hanover Street
Portsmouth, NH 03801–3912
www.boyntoncook.com

Offices and agents throughout the world

© 2000 by Megan Lynn Isaac

The author and publisher wish to thank those who have generously given permission
to reprint borrowed material:

Permission to use cover art granted by Shenandoah Shakespeare, Staunton, Virginia;
original artwork by Chris Cohen.

Library of Congress Cataloging-in-Publication Data

Isaac, Megan Lynn.
    Heirs to Shakespeare : reinventing the Bard in young adult literature /
Megan Lynn Isaac.
        p.   cm. — (Young adult literature series)
    Includes bibliographical references (p.) and index.
    ISBN 0-86709-494-X
    1. Shakespeare, William, 1564–1616—Adaptations—History and criticism.
2. Young adult literature, American—History and criticism.   3. Young adult
literature, English—History and criticism.   4. Shakespeare, William, 1564–1616—
In literature.   I. Title.   II. Young adult literature series (Portsmouth, N.H.).
PR2880.A1 I83   2000
810.9'9283—dc21   99-086192

Consulting editor: Virginia Monseau
Production coordinator: Sonja Chapman
Production service: Lisa Garboski/bookworks
Cover design: Jenny Jensen Greenleaf
Manufacturing: Deanna Richardson

Printed in the United States of America on acid-free paper
04 03 02 01 00   DA   1 2 3 4 5

In memory of my grandmother, Katherine Ray Perine Isaac,
who loved children's books and the theatre.

Contents

Acknowledgments

I used to be amused by other people's acknowledgments—good grief, they were worse than Academy Awards acceptance speeches! Now that I am trying to write my own, I find my perspective has taken a sudden sympathetic shift. Where do I begin? With Dale Harrison, my husband, who learned very quickly that, "How's the book going today, Honey?" was not a good question to ask and made me dinner instead? With Rebecca Barnhouse, who kept insisting I could do it—and read drafts on short notice? With my editor, Virginia Monseau, who first convinced me my ideas were worth presenting in a book? With Youngstown State University for providing me with some reassigned time so I could focus more easily on my writing? With the generous and good humored participants on the listserv child_lit who suggested many of the texts discussed in this volume? With my own English teachers who introduced me to the excitement of Shakespeare and Renaissance drama—Madeleine Lief, Bertrand Goldgar, Robert Watson, and A. R. Braunmuller? With my parents, Barbara and Walt Isaac, who read books to me, bought me books, and let me check out as many books from the library as I could carry? With Heminges and Condell for having the foresight to gather and preserve Shakespeare's plays in the First Folio in 1623? It is so easy to get carried away and so hard to know where to end.

Introduction

Throughout the past decade or more, debates over middle school and high school Language Arts curricula have intensified. Some argue vociferously in favor of the classics, citing the importance of tradition, a shared cultural background, and a suspicion that the classroom is the only place where students are likely to meet canonical works. Others view the goals of education differently, asserting the importance of introducing students to culturally relevant material and the critical need to develop a love of learning through reading. Both sides present a convincing case, but with such fervor that the debate sometimes seems to invite exclusivity and polarization. Either William Shakespeare, Charles Dickens, and Jane Austen are championed or Robert Cormier, Cynthia Voigt, and Mildred Taylor are favored. Forging weak compromises, the advocates of young adult literature teach *Romeo and Juliet* as a sop to the traditionalist, and the champions of the canon offer *The Chocolate War* as an end-of-the-year treat to departing students who are so anxious to embrace summer vacation they nearly have to be stapled into their seats anyway. What both factions have so often failed to see, however, is that even these seemingly diverse literary traditions are inseparably linked— they inform and comment on each other through a literary technique often labeled *intertextuality*. Teaching Shakespeare and young adult literature as complementary aspects of literary, artistic, and social history offers an opportunity to inform and strengthen both approaches to education and curriculum design, even to reveal that they are two sides of the same coin.

The purpose of this book is to illustrate explicitly how canonical literature, especially Shakespeare, informs the characters, plots, and interpretations of many recent books for middle- and high-school-aged audiences. And, perhaps, even more importantly, to demonstrate that these popular novels and Shakespearean plays reveal multiple layers of meaning when read in tandem. Each may be a good story by itself, but knowing both texts makes them even better. Every new piece of literature has the potential to transform all the art that preceded it. These transformations maintain our connection to the past at the same time as we adapt the old to fit the circumstances of a new day. Teaching students to view literature through such a lens highlights the modernity and contemporary meaning of even the oldest authors and stories.

An extraordinary quantity of materials currently available serves to link young readers and Shakespeare. Chapter 1, "Retelling the Tales: Examining Editions of Shakespeare," helps orient readers new to the field to the history of adaptations and revisions of Shakespeare's plays aimed at children and young adults. Chapter 2, "Picturing Shakespeare: Illustrated Editions for Readers of All Ages," explores the ways picture book editions and other visually rich versions of Shakespeare provide an interpretation of the plays akin, in some ways, to the interpretations provided by live theatrical performances. I demonstrate how the scenes an illustrator chooses to represent the style of art selected, and the palette of colors employed, all work together both to forefront a specific vision of a play and to eliminate other potential understandings of the story. Students who compare and contrast several visual interpretations of a play, even in picture books, can reach a greater understanding of the complexity and endless possibilities of Shakespearean drama.

Chapter 3, "Shakespeare's World: Looking at the Renaissance Through Historical Fiction," invites readers to expand their appreciation of Shakespeare's plays by understanding the world in which they were first produced and enjoyed. I introduce and discuss those aspects of the sixteenth and seventeenth centuries most likely to appeal to young readers, like the ravages produced by the plague, the life of traveling actors, the very common experience of working as a servant, and the rigors of apprenticeship as they appear in historically informative young adult novels. Jill Paton Walsh's *A Parcel of Patterns* (1983), Geraldine McCaughrean's *A Little Lower Than the Angels* (1987), Gary Blackwood's *The Shakespeare Stealer* (1998), Susan Cooper's *The King of Shadows* (1999), and Harriet Graham's *A Boy and His Bear* (1994) offer particularly meaningful insights into the period.

Chapters 1 through 3 should be of value to all readers, but the next six chapters each focus on one or two plays and explore the textual interplay between popular Shakespearean texts and a small collection of young adult novels. Chapter 4 explores *Romeo and Juliet* as reconsidered in David Belbin's *Love Lessons* (1998), Avi's *Romeo and Juliet Together (and Alive!) at Last* (1987), Anne McCaffrey's *The Ship Who Sang* (1969), and Geoffrey Trease's *Cue for Treason* (1941). Chapter 5 looks at *Hamlet* as adapted and revised by Katherine Paterson in *Bridge to Terabithia* (1977), Laura Sonnenmark in *Something's Rotten in the State of Maryland* (1990), and Lois Duncan in *Killing Mr. Griffin* (1978). Chapter 6 investigates *Macbeth* with Madeleine L'Engle's *A Wrinkle in Time* (1962), Penelope Lively's *The Whispering Knights* (1971) and *The House in Norham Gardens* (1974), Kate Gilmore's *Enter Three Witches* (1990), Terry Pratchett's *Wyrd Sisters* (1988), Welwyn Wilton Katz's *Come Like Shadows*

(1993), and Sharon M. Draper's *Tears of a Tiger* (1994). Chapter 7 looks at *The Tempest* as presented in Madeleine L'Engle's *A Wrinkle in Time* (1962), Zibby Oneal's *In Summer Light* (1985), Tad Williams' *Caliban's Hour* (1994), and Dennis Covington's *Lizard* (1991).

In these chapters I discuss how modern authors of young adult literature borrow and adapt characters and plot lines from Shakespeare's plays. I demonstrate how these adaptations change or inflect traditional interpretations of Shakespeare's plays and the purposes such changes serve. Comparisons of these canonical plays and contemporary novels will help readers understand how literature creates an ongoing discussion, which crosses continents as well as centuries. All of these texts are rich in allusions—references to characters, events, and language used in an earlier book or play. These echoes or links between a newer text and its predecessors are what literary critics mean when they use the term *intertextuality*. Recognizing intertextuality helps readers perceive literature not only as an artistic phenomenon, but also as a mode of history and an approach to understanding social and cultural changes and continuities—especially in arenas of immediate significance to young readers, like parental relationships, romantic experiences, and violent confrontations. Most importantly, these chapters help bridge the divide between two of the most popular and contentious approaches to curriculum development and educational goals by illustrating the importance of and interrelationships among Shakespearean plays and young adult novels.

Chapter 8, "*Othello* and *The Merchant of Venice:* Challenging the Status Quo," continues the work of the previous chapters but extends the questions raised there by looking at two plays that deal with thorny issues of particular pertinence to modern society—racism and anti-Semitism. Here I focus on Louise Plummer's *The Unlikely Romance of Kate Bjorkman* (1995), Farrukh Dhondy's *Black Swan* (1993), Julius Lester's *Othello: A Novel* (1995), and Kate Gilmore's *Jason and the Bard* (1993). I also compare the ways children's editions of Shakespeare have presented Shylock over the past two centuries.

Chapter 9, "A Tragedy in the Classroom: The Disappearance of Comedies and Histories," discusses the genres of Shakespeare's work least familiar to young readers. Focusing on two plays, *A Midsummer Night's Dream* and *Richard III*, this chapter presents strategies to introduce comedies and tragedies to young readers. Marilyn Singer's *The Course of True Love Never Did Run Smooth* (1983) and Terry Pratchett's *Lords and Ladies* (1992) highlight the gleeful and confusing ways love plays tricks on us all at the same time as they do homage to one of Shakespeare's best-loved comedies. Stephanie Tolan's *The Face in the Mirror* (1998) and John Ford's *Dragon Waiting* (1983) provide the contemporary approaches for understanding *Richard III*.

A brief note about terms: I think of the material discussed in this book as falling into three rough categories. The first of these are the *originals*—texts authored by Shakespeare. Although, we know that many editors, printers, and directors have tampered with or shaped these texts since Shakespeare wrote them, they are, in practical terms, the closest we can get to his original writing. The second category consists of *children's editions*. These are versions of Shakespeare's plays, re-shaped for younger readers. The editors or authors of these versions (both terms are used) may have made changes in the length of the text, the vocabulary, and the style of the story. Generally, these versions aspire to make Shakespeare's work more accessible to young readers, not to change it, interpret it, or comment on it (though change, interpretation, and commentary are inescapable effects of creating a children's edition). Children's editions by themselves will seem inappropriately simplistic for most young adult readers, but as ancillary materials they can serve as wonderful tools for exploring Shakespeare's plays and the ways our culture has responded to them. The last category of texts are those I refer to as *revisions* or *reinterpretations* of Shakespeare's plays. These texts, usually novels, use Shakespeare as a springboard. Writers of these works faithfully adopt aspects of Shakespeare's plays and un-apologetically add new characters, new settings, and new events to the tales. Some revisions are very subtle and may go completely unrec-ognized by readers not already well-versed in Shakespeare. Other re-visions make very overt use of a play and repeatedly draw a reader's attention to the ways the author has intertextually adapted and exper-imented with Shakespeare's materials. Many young adult novelists re-interpret Shakespeare with thought-provocative flair.

Young Adult Novel Reference List

Arranged alphabetically below is a quick summary of the Shakespearean plays explored in this book and the young adult novels discussed in detail that revise or reinterpret them. Novels discussed only briefly are not included here.

Hamlet

Duncan, L. (1978). *Killing Mr. Griffin.*

Paterson, K. (1977). *Bridge to Terabithia.*

Sonnenmark, L. (1990). *Something's Rotten in the State of Maryland.*

Macbeth

Draper, S.M. (1994). *Tears of a Tiger.*

Gilmore, K. (1990). *Enter Three Witches.*

Katz, W.W. (1993). *Come Like Shadows.*

Pratchett, T. (1988). *Wyrd Sisters.*

A Midsummer Night's Dream

Pratchett, T. (1992). *Lords and Ladies.*

Singer, M. (1992). *The Course of True Love Never Did Run Smooth.*

Othello

Dhondy, F. (1993). *Black Swan.*

Gilmore, K. (1993). *Jason and the Bard.*

Lester, J. (1995). *Othello: A Novel.*

Plummer, L. (1995). *The Unlikely Romance of Kate Bjorkman.*

Richard III

Ford, J. (1983). *Dragon Waiting.*

Tolan, S. (1998). *The Face in the Mirror.*

Romeo and Juliet

Avi. (1987). *Romeo and Juliet Together (and Alive!) at Last.*

Belbin, D. (1998). *Love Lessons.*

McCaffrey, A. (1969). *The Ship Who Sang.*

Trease, G. (1941). *Cue for Treason.*

The Tempest

Covington, D. (1991). *Lizard.*

L'Engle, M. (1962). *A Wrinkle in Time.*

Oneal, Z. (1985). *In Summer Light.*

Williams, T. (1994). *Caliban's Hour.*

Noteworthy Historical Fiction for Readers of Shakespeare

Blackwood, G. (1998). *The Shakespeare Stealer.*

Cooper, S. (1999). *The King of Shadows.*

Graham, H. (1994). *A Boy and His Bear.*

McCaughrean, G. (1987). *A Little Lower Than the Angels.*

Walsh, J. P. (1983). *A Parcel of Patterns.*

Chapter One

Retelling the Tales: Examining Editions of Shakespeare

A Brief History

Shakespearean scholars in academia have rarely paid much attention to the editions of Shakespeare published for young people. And one might argue that they have received such a cold or empty reception with good reason. Editors of such texts have sometimes failed to exhibit much in the way of scholarly knowledge about their subject or have subjugated textual authenticity to some other goal—like moral instruction. On the other hand, such behavior on the part of Shakespearean scholars might well be described as painfully shortsighted. Many, perhaps even most, readers of Shakespeare do not first encounter his plays in the thoughtfully emended, carefully arranged, and helpfully footnoted editions churned out by Oxford, Cambridge, Arden, or the other major players in the Shakespeare industry. Instead, they meet these plays in children's and school editions.

For well over a century, Shakespeare has been a part of educational curricula. In nineteenth century England (and to a lesser extent in the United States), at least a passing knowledge of Shakespeare was necessary to make even the smallest claims toward being an educated individual. In 1870 the British Parliament created the state school system, and Shakespeare played a significant role in the newly devised subject of English Literature (Taylor 1989, 194). Shakespeare's centrality within these curricula has wavered and, by many accounts, waned over the years, but the plays retain a certain prominence. In a report issued in 1989 by the British Department of Education and Science, educational evaluators concluded, "almost everyone agrees that his work should be represented in a National Curriculum. Shakespeare's plays are so rich that in every age they can produce fresh meanings and even those who deny his universality agree on his cultural importance" (qtd. in Allen 1991, 41). Concerns about the declining achievement of American school children (warranted or not) have also led many educators and politicians to look to the past for answers. In a pronouncement describing a program proposal for American national education standards, Secretary of Education Richard Riley announced in 1997 that every high school graduate would study at least two of Shakespeare's plays as part of the curriculum. And a peek at the contents of any well-stocked public library or mass-market bookstore reveals the continued prominence of Shakespearean editions for children.

Given this popularity, a brief overview of the history of children's editions of Shakespeare may better enable teachers, as well as students, to understand the strengths and weaknesses of these volumes. Within a hundred years of his death, Shakespeare had so grown in prominence that the literary critic Lewis Theobald was able to claim that in England very few home libraries or collections of books were without a copy of his plays (qtd. in Thompson 1997, 1). Yet, Shakespeare's plays contain many sexually suggestive scenes, a variety of oaths (including irreverent references to God and Christ), and numerous examples of immoral behavior. Many conservative teachers and cultural critics felt these "slips" or indiscretions in Shakespeare's plays presented problems for women and children. Ladies and young readers might not understand these scenes, and it would be embarrassing for men to have to explain them. Or worse yet, they might understand them completely and that would prove that the ladies and children were not as "pure" or "innocent" as they ought to be!

In 1807 two different Shakespearean scholars developed a solution to the problem of Shakespeare's indelicacies. Henrietta Bowdler published a volume of twenty plays entitled *The Family Shakespeare,* the first edition of Shakespeare prepared with young readers in mind. As she carefully explained in her preface, she added nothing to the plays, but removed many speeches "in which Shakespeare has been tempted to purchase laughter at the price of decency" in order to enable young readers of both sexes to make an acquaintance with Shakespeare without raising "a blush on the cheek of modesty" (qtd. in Thompson, 47). She was herself a fifty-three-year-old spinster, and women of her position were not supposed to understand or acknowledge sexual innuendoes or vulgar language, let alone scour twenty plays searching out such words and phrases. Ironically, in order to preserve her good reputation, Henrietta had to publish her volume under her brother's name,

Thomas Bowdler, and until a few years ago scholars did not know she was the true editor of the text. In later years her brother and several other family members published new editions of *The Family Shakespeare,* some more heavily edited than others. Due to their work, the word *bowdlerize* has entered the English language as a term for prudish expurgation.

Mary and Charles Lambs' collaborative rendition of twenty plays into prose stories in *Tales from Shakespeare,* also published in 1807, presents a different approach to making Shakespeare appropriate for young readers. These tales are, apparently, the first significant narrative retellings of Shakespeare for a young audience. The Lambs felt that since children are more familiar with the style and conventions of stories than dramas, prose retellings would be both more easily comprehended and more appealing to young readers. The Lambs described their work not as a substitute for Shakespeare, but as a kind of bait that would first foster a child's taste for the plays and later tempt the child to seek out the originals as soon as his or her literary skills and parents would permit. The influence of these tales should not be underestimated. Reprinted more than thirty times during the nineteenth century, the Lambs' text is nearly canonical in stature itself (Taylor 208). It is frequently used as an introduction to Shakespeare not only in English-speaking countries, but in translation in places as distant as Japan (Bottoms 1996, 74). These tales, like many of the nineteenth century versions, were intended chiefly for young girls, since boys usually were, as the Lambs themselves said in their introduction,

> permitted the use of their father's libraries at a much earlier age than girls [were] . . . and, therefore, instead of recommending these Tales to the perusal of young gentlemen who can read them so much better in the originals, their kind assistance is rather requested in explaining to their sisters such parts as are hardest for them to understand. (Lamb viii)

Some of the other early adaptations for young readers with less historical influence than the work of the Bowdlers and the Lambs include Caroline Maxwell's *The Juvenile Edition of Shakespeare: Adapted to the Capacities of Youth* (1828), Elizabeth Macauley's *Tales of the Drama* (1833), Mary Seamer's *Shakespeare's Stories Simply Told* (1880), Amelia E. Barr's *The Young People of Shakespeare's Dramas: For Youthful Readers* (1882), Adelaide Sim's *Phoebe's Shakespeare* (1894), M. Surtees Townsend's *Stories from Shakespeare* (1899), and Ada B. Stidolph's *The Children's Shakespeare* (1902) (Hunt 105 and Thompson xv). The quantity of these adaptations attests to the popularity of children's editions.

Two other early editors, however, merit a little bit more attention. Mary Crowden Clarke's five volume work *The Girlhood of Shakespeare's*

Heroines (1850–1852) takes a different approach to bringing Shakespeare to young readers. Clarke works from the premise that children most enjoy stories about people their own age. Instead of rewriting Shakespeare's comedies and tragedies with their adult protagonists, she imagines what the childhood of Shakespeare's characters, especially his heroines, might have been like. Clarke imagines a young Kate, from the *Taming of the Shrew,* who throws rocks at a young boy and knocks him unconscious. Her rash impatience, especially with members of the other sex, shows itself from her youth. All fifteen of the tales include vivid, and often melodramatic, foreshadowings of the Shakespearean plays. Clarke's work has provoked a great deal of humor and scorn from Shakespearean scholars. As literary criticism, it doesn't have a great deal to offer, but Clarke was no amateur—she was an innovator. In 1844–1845 she produced the first *Concordance* to Shakespeare. A concordance is a cross between a dictionary and an index—a reader looks up a word and the concordance lists every place in every Shakespeare play in which it occurs. Variations of Shakespeare concordances are still being produced today, although computer searches now make such scholarship much simpler to manage. Similarly, Clarke's *The Girlhood of Shakespeare's Heroines* should be seen as the first of many, many narrative reinterpretations of Shakespeare's plays. In 1991, Jane Smiley won the Pulitzer Prize for *A Thousand Acres,* a novel that reimagines *King Lear* as the tale of an aging Iowa farmer. This wonderful novel is a clear descendant of Clarke's tales, as are many of the young adult novels explored in Chapters 4 through 9.

Finally, Edith Nesbit (also known as E. Bland) deserves mention. During the early decades of the twentieth century Nesbit made a reputation for herself as one of the most popular writers of children's literature famous for titles like *The Would-Be-Goods* (1901), *The Phoenix and the Carpet* (1904), and *The Railway Children* (1908). Earlier in her career, however, Nesbit published *The Children's Shakespeare* (1900), which was later followed by several other variants of Shakespeare's tales. Two versions of these volumes have been recently reprinted. In some ways they epitomize the best and the worst of early editions of children's Shakespeare. Nesbit admits to being deeply indebted to the Lambs' text, which was published nearly a full century before her own. Like the Lambs, Nesbit assumes that unmediated Shakespeare is a particular challenge for young female readers. Although she doesn't claim that her tales are only for girls, the subtext of her introduction reveals that young women are her target audience:

> It was evening. The fire burned brightly in the inn parlor. We had been that day to see Shakespeare's house, and I had told the children all that I could about him and his work. Now they were sitting by the table, poring over a big volume of the Master's plays lent them by the landlord. (5)

Much to the author's dismay, however, the children soon begin to complain about the difficulty of the text. A dialogue ensues revealing "the children" to be girls named Iris and Rosamund. The author consents to ease their frustration by writing a simple version of the plays for them—a version that concentrates on the stories. Like many of her nineteenth-century predecessors, Nesbit also inserts moral instructions into the tales. Juliet's life, she intones, would have turned out differently if she had spoken out and told her father the truth when he ordered her to marry Paris (16). Lying to one's parents, the author less than subtly implies, only brings disaster. Like the Lambs' text, Nesbit's work is readily available, conveniently enabling modern students to compare how Shakespeare was presented to young readers at the turn of the nineteenth and twentieth centuries as well as at the opening of the twenty-first century.

Most of the recent versions of Shakespeare for children are more equitable in their imagined audience, aiming at young male readers as well as young female readers, and less inclined to insert overt moral precepts. Marchette Chute's *Stories from Shakespeare* (1956), Beverley Birch's three volume *Shakespeare's Stories* (1988), and Leon Garfield's two volume *Shakespeare Stories* (1995) also struggle to make the original plays available to younger audiences. These collections are only a small sample of the retellings of Shakespeare available in libraries and bookstores. Bottoms' 1996 study of the market for children's editions of Shakespeare revealed upwards of thirty versions since 1807, and this count includes only collections (74). Additionally, there are many single-text editions and picture books based on Shakespeare, most of which have been produced during the past century.

Evaluating Editions of Shakespeare

The use of Shakespeare in literature for young people raises a number of interesting questions about the place of Shakespeare in our culture and the function of children's and young adult literature as a tool for socialization and indoctrination. Traditionally, children's literature is a conservative genre. In order for the texts to reach their intended audience, they must be purchased, reviewed, and approved by parents, teachers, librarians, or other adult arbitrators of culture and values. On one level, Shakespeare's name appears to authenticate a text within a patriarchal culture. These collections or editions introduce young audiences to one of the most admired and respected authors in the Western canon. And, since sophisticated children's literature is always aware of multiple audiences (child readers and adult readers), such texts reward the adult reader with a sense of his or her own sophistication through the recognition and appreciation of Shakespeare. The texts make the adult reader feel well-educated and suggest that they will prepare a younger reader to become well-educated too.

But any retelling or adaptation of Shakespeare's plays necessarily entails an interpretation, and, as much of the criticism of the past few decades has emphasized, there are no truly innocent or apolitical interpretations. Some editors, like Henrietta Bowdler and the Lambs, have been relatively overt in articulating the forms or intentions of their interpretations. These editors claimed to be driven by decorum, a desire to select what might be most proper and "to remove every thing that could give just offence to the religious and virtuous mind" (Bowdler qtd. in Taylor, 207). Other editors claim only to be condensing or simplifying the stories and the language in which they are told in order to facilitate a child's introduction to the plays. These editors seem less aware of or at least less interested in examining the interpretive consequences of their choices.

Some of the decisions that editors of Shakespeare for young people must make are more sweeping than others. Perhaps the first decision faced is which plays to include and which to exclude entirely. Although quite a few editors, like Marchette Chute, have produced a virtually complete collection of Shakespeare, including thirty-six plays, a condensation of the canon to approximately twenty plays is more typical. Plays with difficult topics, like *Antony and Cleopatra*, with its thematic exploration of adultery and betrayal, or *Titus Andronicus*, with its representations of sexual violence, dismemberment, and cannibalism, are often among those plays excluded from collections for young people. The history plays, in many ways the least plot-driven of Shakespeare's dramas, are also often represented only in small numbers.

Editors of Shakespeare for the young need to make other decisions about narrative form rarely faced by traditional editors. Although his soaring poetry is one of the aspects of Shakespeare's dramas most frequently lauded, it is also one of the reasons so many editors seem to feel a need to produce special versions for children. Poetry is presumed to be too difficult for young readers. Most editions eschew Shakespeare's verse in favor of a prose retelling. Some editors carefully incorporate fragments of the original dialogue and poetry into their versions in order to preserve, as far as possible, an authentic Shakespearean flavor. Others choose to rewrite the text entirely in the hope of avoiding the schizophrenic tone that so often results from interspersing the words and style of a sixteenth century author with those of a twentieth century editor.

Lois Burdett's recent editions of five plays created in collaboration with her elementary school students are among the few children's versions of the plays that attempt to use poetry. Her edition of *Macbeth* (1996) begins:

I convey you to Scotland of yesteryear,
A place locked in combat, cruel and severe.
A country called Norway sent troops 'cross the sea.
The Scottish fought back to keep their land free.
Smoke and fire thickened the skies;
The air thundered with fierce battle cries.
The very ground shuddered with fright;
It really was a dreadful night.
As the men battled with sword and shield,
Grey shadows appeared on the distant field.
"When shall we three meet again?
In thunder, lightning or in rain?" (6–7)

A purist may well shudder at the rows of rattling rhymes and the pounding insistence of the meter, but at the same time Burdett gives her young readers a kind of aesthetic credit that few of her predecessors have acknowledged—children can appreciate and understand poetry. Students who first meet Shakespeare in verse, even if that verse is stilted or jarring, will be less surprised when they eventually come to the original texts and meet blank verse than students who have only read Shakespeare as narrative stories little different in structure and format from fairy tales.

Perhaps even more importantly, by maintaining the poetic form of the dramas, Burdett also better maintains the sense of multiple perspectives and competing points of view crucial to dramas. Plays, unlike novels, do not usually have an overt narrator to lead and guide the audience. For example, audiences watching *Hamlet* have the opportunity to hear about the old King's death from several different characters—and if the actors are charismatic enough, each character may seem compelling. Editors who choose prose narrations over poetic or dramatic forms inescapably privilege their own voice over that of any of the characters. The process of turning the dialogue of a play into the narrative of a story forces the editor to take interpretive positions. There are no stage directions in *Hamlet* to explain how King Claudius should deliver his lines, but if an adaptor of the play tells readers that Claudius spoke "slyly," "with a sneer," or "in an oily voice," readers receive a very specific message about how to interpret the King. Subtleties and complexities of character are lost. On the other hand, readers of a version that retains dramatic form must decide for themselves whether King Claudius speaks gently, hisses, or thunders his words. Furthermore, Janet Bottoms argues that narrative versions of Shakespeare's plays always align themselves with the main character (which, in some plays, entails making a choice about who deserves to be designated as "the main character") and accept unquestioningly this character's perspective on and judgments about all the other characters and events in the drama (81–83). Shakespeare, or at least those who advocate the study of his work, has frequently been accused of representing a narrowly patriarchal world view in the plays, and regardless of the value of this criticism, it seems worth noting that the prose versions aimed at young people by their very structure only intensify this phenomenon. Dramatic form almost always leaves more room for interpretation than narrative form.

Finally, changing Shakespeare's plays from dramatic form to prose form usually forces editors to make structural changes. The multiple plots, which are a highlight of so many of the plays in performance, seem to be much less appealing to editors of Shakespeare for young readers. Some editors simply remove secondary plot lines in the interest of brevity. Others untangle the plot lines and tell them sequentially in hope of clarifying the story for younger audiences (Bottoms 78).

Young people's editions of Shakespeare are, almost by definition, abridged versions of the plays. Many would argue that to choose material, as any editor or adaptor must, is, inherently, to lose things—not only rich language and descriptions, but ambiguities and complexities as well. Historically, these necessities have led most scholars and critics to dismiss children's editions of the plays. Yet, the choices these editors make are not unique. Professional actors, directors, filmmakers, textual editors—not to mention classroom teachers—also make choices and preference one interpretation (or at best two or three) every time they present a Shakespearean drama to an audience. Every reading is an interpretation, and it is important to take note of what kinds of interpretations are being presented to the developing Shakespearean audiences—children and young adults.

Of course, many classrooms have used and will continue to use one of the standard editions of the plays, often as presented within an anthology of literature. But the popularity of the Bard in the curriculum has fed, if not created, a small sideline within the Shakespearean industry of editions for children. Whether purchased by well-meaning parents or ambitious educators hoping to plant the seed of Shakespearean appreciation, versions of the plays aimed at young readers grow ever more ubiquitous and, happily, provide increasing opportunities for exploring Shakespeare.

Empowering Readers

Editions of Shakespeare for young readers are not without flaws or limitations; in fact, it seems to be one of the conventions of the genre that any editor or adaptor must include a modest acknowledgment that his or her work is no substitute for the Bard. Nonetheless, each editor brazenly goes on to present the work to readers in lieu of Shakespeare's original. Similarly, the defects of children's versions should not be mistaken as an argument for dismissing them. Instead, these flaws can be viewed as a terrific opportunity to enable young readers to become critical readers and astute interpreters of Shakespeare.

Students can read several children's versions of a Shakespeare play and explore the differences among them. Students working with a full Shakespeare play can use one or more of these versions as a meaningful variation on quasi-educational resources like *Cliffs Notes* or *Monarch Notes*. Children's versions can serve as models for students interested in creating their own abridgement or adaptation of a play. They are not a substitute for Shakespeare—at least no more so than any text is a substitute for "real" Shakespeare, which is to say a live performance of a play. Instead, children's versions may be usefully viewed as interpretations of a play and as invitations to further interpretation.

Below is a list of questions readers might consider as they analyze a children's version of Shakespeare. Working through these questions should also help readers develop their own avenues of exploration. Readers including picture book versions in their comparisons may want to consider other questions related to visual interpretations discussed in Chapter 2.

- How does the children's version open? Is the setting or mood different from the original play? What is the effect of these changes?
- Have any characters been eliminated from the play? If so, what role did these characters serve in the original?
- What are the consequences of removing characters from this play?
- Have any scenes been removed or reordered in the play? If so, why has the editor of the children's version moved these scenes?
- Is the children's version in prose or verse?
- What benefits do you see in choosing prose or verse?
- Shakespeare uses soliloquies to tell the audience what a character is thinking. How does the editor of the children's version explore the thoughts of the characters?
- Does the editor of the children's version tell readers more or less of the characters' internal thoughts and feelings?
- Shakespeare gives his actors almost no stage directions. He never says whether an actor should speak the lines angrily or fearfully or sadly. Does the editor of the children's version insert these sorts of directions? How does this help a reader? How does this limit a reader?
- Shakespeare's characters often make sexual innuendoes. Have any of these survived into the children's edition? Do you agree that it is appropriate to remove some or all of this material?

- How much violence do you see in the children's edition? Has the editor done anything to make the violence seem less graphic or less significant? Is the editor emphasizing the terrible consequences of violence more or less than Shakespeare?

- Do you see any main themes or points in the play? Do the main points change depending on what version you read?

- All of Shakespeare's plays have humorous moments. Do you see any comedy in the children's versions?

- When was the version written? Does it reflect the historical period in which it was created? Is Shakespeare always the same, or do the plays change with each generation?

- Do the children's versions increase your understanding of the play? How?

- Do the children's versions limit your understanding of the play? How?

- What assumptions is the editor making about young readers by making changes in the text?

Chapter Two

Picturing Shakespeare: Illustrated Editions for Readers of All Ages

English teachers and literary scholars unceasingly condemn Shakespeare's plays to the greatest of indignities—we insist on reading them. But, as many critics have said before, Shakespeare wrote for the stage, not the page. The most authentic way to get to know Shakespeare's plays is through the experience of live, theatrical performances. Other forms of study may enable us to better appreciate the knotty complexities and soaring imagery of Shakespeare's poetry, but they are still only second-class substitutes for leaning forward with a roomful of other people to smell the smoke of a burning torch, to watch the fragile hands tremble, and to catch the hissing whisper of Lady Macbeth's infamous "Out, damn'd spot! out, I say!" (5.1.35). Virtually all young scholars of Shakespeare find the plays more interesting to watch than to read. So do most adults! While watching a play, unfamiliar character names are immediately forgotten and complex lines fly by unheeded, but many people can still claim with confidence to have understood what happened to whom. The language of the script and the interpretive choices of the actor melt together to create visible meaning.

Ironically, picture books, which may seem the least and most humble of Shakespearean adaptations, bring readers closer in some ways to a theatrical experience than the text-based abridgements and adaptations more frequently offered to young readers. Picture books provide a visual interpretation of the play—much in the way a theatrical performance does.

Picture Books as Interpretations

Experienced theater-going audiences frequently exchange critiques of productions. One person may prefer Kevin Kline's performance as Hamlet, but another may rave about a different production starring Val Kilmer. One person really only enjoys performances using Elizabethan period dress, but another loves to see Shakespeare updated with Victorian costumes or futuristic apparel. The points of comparison and discussion for experienced audiences are endless because these fortunate theater patrons recognize that the more ways they experience a play, the more they learn about it. Even a stumbling and misguided performance of a play enables many Shakespeare fans to better see what they value in the play simply by its absence.

Unfortunately, most young students of Shakespeare do not have the theatrical background to enable a discussion of the merits and failings of various productions. The availability of filmed versions makes some comparison possible—students can watch Lawrence Olivier, Derek Jacobi, and Kenneth Branagh all play Hamlet and argue with Gertrude or confront the unexpected spectacle of Ophelia in her grave—but watching the entirety of three versions of *Hamlet* is rarely possible (and not even usually desirable when time is short). Illustrated editions of picture books can, however, provide a very realistic shortcut for visual interpretation of a play.

All directors of stage and film productions make decisions. Many of Shakespeare's plays exist in more than one version, and decisions have to be made about which text to use, how many lines to cut, and whether to rearrange scenes. Casting decisions also shape an interpretation as well. Will Hamlet be seventeen or thirty-four years old? Choices about costumes, sets, props, and lighting also must be made.

Authors and illustrators of picture book adaptations of Shakespeare make similar sets of choices. Like any other writer who revises or edits Shakespeare, the author must decide how much of the play to keep and what elements of the story to emphasize. Some writers strive to present a balanced overview of the entire play, making judicious cuttings from every scene. More commonly, writers prefer to forefront a subset of the characters. Not surprisingly, younger characters are often emphasized in editions for children, and plot lines treating family and love are frequently given precedence over those concerned with politics and government. The decisions the author makes are not right or wrong, they are interpretive.

Illustrators make the same sorts of interpretive choices in the visual domain. They make decisions about how a character will look—blonde hair or red. More importantly, though, illustrators set the mood of the adaptation and select the focal points of the story through their selection of which scenes to illustrate. For example, an illustrated version of *Romeo and Juliet* can be bathed in blood or moonlight. An illustrator who chooses a palette of pastel shades to portray Romeo and Juliet meeting at the Capulet masque, whispering on the balcony, and weeping in the tomb will create a very different interpretation of the play than one who with bold streaks of red and black makes the opening street brawl, the fight between Tybalt and Mercutio, and Romeo's duel with Paris the illustrative centerpieces of the adaptation. Of course, many illustrators choose to portray elements of both the romance and the violence of the play, but no illustrator has the luxury of portraying every scene from every viewpoint in every artistic style, and so, like a director or even an actor, illustrators are forced, ultimately, into a series of interpretive decisions.

Picture book interpretations of the plays provide students of varying levels with the tools to begin thoughtful discussions of Shakespeare's plays. Students can easily compare two or more illustrators' interpretations of a character, a scene, or an entire play. Articulating why one artist's vision appeals more than another forces "readers" of these illustrations to explore their own assumptions about how a character or scene is "supposed" to look. Discussing the choices they would make if producing an illustrated version of Shakespeare can work to empower students in regard to their own interpretive understanding of the plays. Recognizing that adults regularly produce extremely varied interpretations of the plays helps students to understand that drama is inherently collaborative and flexible—there are not "right" answers to questions provoked by the plays as much as there are well-designed ones.

Visual interpretive tools like picture books are also particularly helpful when exploring controversial or contentious elements of Shakespeare's plays. Caliban, a character from *The Tempest,* makes a stunning case study in the power and variety of dramatic interpretation. Over the centuries Caliban has been discussed by critics and presented by actors as an ill-shapen demon, an ignorant savage, and an enslaved native islander, to name just a few of his many guises. Illustrated versions of the play for young readers also struggle to find a vision of this character. Arthur Rackham's illustrations from 1899, which accompany Mary and Charles Lambs' classic retellings of Shakespeare (1807), portray Caliban as a beast with a sinuous body, scales, tail, fangs, and whiskers. Michael Foreman's illustrations in Leon Garfield's (1985) collection of stories present a comic vision of Caliban. With his green skin, pug-nosed snout, and crooked horn, this Caliban seems unlikely to be considered a serious threat. An even more recent Caliban, as portrayed by Gennady Spirin in Ann Keay Beneduce's (1996) picture book adaptation of the play, is hairy, heavily muscled, and small skulled, but crested like a lizard or Gila monster. Nonetheless, his watchful eyes warn readers that he is a force to be reckoned with, even if his shape is not entirely familiar or human. Students can further explore the ways Caliban has been portrayed by searching for photographs or costume sketches from stage and film performances of the play.

Two Case Studies

Two recent picture book interpretations of Shakespeare use illustration to interpret and expand the stories in complex and thoughtful ways. *The Tempest* as retold by Beneduce with illustrations by Spirin focuses the retelling on the romance between Miranda and Ferdinand and on Prospero's shift from vengeance to forgiveness. Beneduce, like many of the editors discussed in the previous chapter, eliminates most of the action of the subplots. Margaret Early makes similar choices in *Romeo and Juliet* (1998). The tragic romance of the two star-crossed lovers becomes a vehicle for promoting forgiveness and peace in Verona. Most of the wry humor and secondary brawls are eliminated to redefine the focus of the tale for picture book format.

Beneduce's text strikes a memorable balance between a modern narrative and Shakespeare's famous verse by incorporating both elements. She tells the story in colorful and appealing prose that reassures young audiences with the comfortable familiarity of fairy tale cadences and motifs. Her version begins, "Once upon a time there was an enchanted island, a green and lovely place, set in the great sea that lies between Europe and Africa. The air was filled with the sounds of music and the fragrance of flowers" (Beneduce 3). Yet, at the same time she preserves the linguistic melody of the play by incorporating some of the most lyrical and memorable passages in textual insets framed amid the illustrations. Two of Ariel's songs, along with three famous and oft-quoted passages from Prospero, Caliban, and the goddesses, are all presented in this fashion as well. Beneduce's decision to forefront Caliban's speech is particularly interesting, since his character is all but eliminated from her version of the play. Like many readers and audiences before her, Beneduce seems uncomfortable with the ambiguities embedded in Caliban's character—he speaks with both beauty and malice, he inspires both pity and revulsion. Beneduce admires his language enough to retain, even to frame, parts of it in her text, but at the same time the prose narration denies Caliban's complexity and simply refers to him as an evil, ugly, inhuman monster. Most of his scenes are cut entirely from this version of *The Tempest*. The resolution Beneduce arrives at, to keep the poetry but to omit the speaker, is both telling and frustrating. Nonetheless, Beneduce's decision to keep some of the original Shakespearean verse ensures that young readers of this picture book can become familiar with both an understanding of the story line and with some of the most famous language in the play.

Beneduce admits in her afterword that her revisions sometimes "drastically altered" Shakespeare's original. Perhaps this is nowhere more true than in her treatment of the moral ambiguities of power in the play. In Shakespeare's drama, when the magician Prospero finds himself shipwrecked on the island with his infant daughter Miranda, he enslaves the island's two original inhabitants, Caliban and Ariel. Shakespeare provokes us to wonder whether Prospero is caring for Caliban and Ariel or abusing them. He makes his audiences struggle to decide whether Prospero is an admirable leader or a mean-spirited tyrant. Beneduce clarifies and simplifies Prospero's relationships with Caliban and Ariel to make them more palatable and less conflicted for modern readers. She has made the decision to interpret Prospero as a hero and presents him without qualification or quibble. Readers of Shakespeare's play who share Beneduce's vision of Prospero will find her interpretation unremarkable; those who view Prospero with alarm or suspicion may find Beneduce's vision of the play quite provocative.

One particularly knotty ambiguity within Shakespeare's drama concerns Prospero's renunciation of his magic. In the play, even after he claims to have buried his wizard's staff and drowned his books of enchantments, Prospero promises the assembled company to provide them with a journey home, free from storms or troubles. This extravagant offer suggests that, despite his promise to destroy the tools of his trade, not all of his magical powers have been abandoned. Beneduce finesses this plot point in her picture book by having a faithful Ariel offer "to use his own enchantments to bring the ship safely across the sea and back to Naples" (28). In Beneduce's version, Prospero becomes a much more trustworthy and uncomplicated character.

Finally, Miranda becomes a less interesting character in the picture book version of the story. The conflict between loyalties she struggles against in Shakespeare's play when she finds herself forced to choose between her old love for her father and her new love for Ferdinand is missing in Beneduce's reduced version of the story. Similarly, the energetic joy or, perhaps, the glorious absence of decorum that she displays in the play disappears. Shakespeare lets Miranda turn convention on its head when she proposes marriage to Ferdinand. In the picture book readers get a much more traditional wedding proposal. Ferdinand asks Miranda, "Will you be my bride?" (16).

Undoubtedly the most interesting aspect of Beneduce and Spirin's book is not, however, the textual interpretation of the play, but the innovative artwork. Instead of simply illustrating the play, Spirin draws upon the conventions and styles of Renaissance art, especially Italian influences, in the illustrations. Many of the pages are constructed as panels and triptychs, like those commissioned to decorate churches and the homes of the nobility during the Renaissance. Similarly, Spirin uses very little perspective in his drawings—the characters look flat, sometimes pasted against a backdrop. The pictures concentrate on rich details of clothing and delicate silhouettes. Small, round inset illustrations—especially when they focus on the faces of the characters—are reminiscent of Elizabethan "miniatures"—a form of portraiture highly valued in the Renaissance and epitomized in the work of artists like Nicholas Hilliard, who was a contemporary of Shakespeare. The muted tones of red, blue, green, and brown create a sense of the elegance of the world Spirin is illustrating.

The pencil and watercolor techniques allow the artist both to refine precise details in the scenes of love and human interaction and to melt foregrounds seamlessly into backgrounds in the scenes of mystery and magical intervention. The varied layout of the text also invites readers to spend as much time considering the artistic rendering of the tale as the textual component. Full-page and double-page illustrative spreads are interspersed among pages of text and pages of framed and illuminated quotations. Beneduce and Spirin's version of *The Tempest* is not simply a child's book; the complexity of the art invites young adult readers to interpret the tale visually as well as textually. While readers of this version of *The Tempest* are unlikely to learn much about what the play might look like on the stage, they will learn what late sixteenth and early seventeenth century audiences would have recognized as high art and visual splendor.

Early's *Romeo and Juliet* also uses a highly stylized artistic vision of the play to enhance a reader's interpretation of the story. With only six colors of paint (two reds, two yellows, and two blues) and highlights in luminous gold, Early's book recalls the illuminated manuscripts of the Middle Ages. Each page of text is bordered with an intricate pattern of delicate diamonds, triangles, or vines and is accompanied by an illustration even more richly patterned. Wallpapers, tiled floors, elaborate gowns, detailed bed-hangings, and leafy trees are each rendered in exquisite detail. A careful attention to architectural forms (archways, windows, columns, and ceiling beams) further enhances a very measured sense of depth in these paintings. Early's human figures, on the other hand, are all quite static, almost one-dimensional. Romeo and Juliet seem almost doll-like figures posed against a background of striking complexity. While this description might seem like a criticism were Early's paintings gracing the wall of a museum, as accompaniments to Shakespeare's play this style seems poignantly appropriate. Romeo and Juliet are simple lovers caught up in a conflict much larger than themselves and betrayed by complex coincidences far beyond their powers of prediction.Their environment is, in these illustrations, appropriately more elaborate and powerful than the two young lovers themselves.

Although the art of Early's volume invites thoughtful scrutiny, the text of Early's version of *Romeo and Juliet* suggests this retelling of Shakespeare's play may be best suited for readers first being introduced to the story. Early tells the tale in clear and familiar prose. The book opens, "Once upon a time, in the fair city of Verona, lived two noble families, the Montagues and the Capulets. These great households possessed everything that life could offer, but there was no peace between them, for each hated the other worse than death." Readers frightened by horror stories about the complexity or incomprehensibility of Shakespearean verse certainly won't find anything to dismay them in these simple cadences. Like Beneduce, Early uses structures familiar from fairy and folk tales to put her readers at ease.

Similarly, Early eliminates many of Shakespeare's characters and the careful layering of conflicts that supports his play. The reflections and commentary of servants, princes, priests, and citizens that round out and enrich Shakespeare's drama are reduced to passing shadows in Early's version. Here, the attention is almost always on the unquestioned love of Romeo and Juliet. Shakespeare's play frequently highlights the haste of Romeo and Juliet's infatuation and interrogates their courses of action. In Early's version, however, the lovers are emblems of sincere love whose actions are above reproach. To enable this romanticized interpretation of the play, Early has made important choices both in her text and illustrations. For example, Romeo is all but relieved of bloodshed. His enraged murder of Tybalt occurs in a single blow. His murder of the rival suitor Paris never occurs at all. Similarly, only one illustration in the entire book illustrates the violence of Verona. In this picture, a small pool of blood trickles from Mercutio's fallen body, and Romeo stands with sword drawn while Tybalt rushes forward to impale himself on his opponent's blade. Romeo is a gentle lover victimized by the violence of Verona, not a participant in its bloody ideologies. Early's book is a tale more about beauty than death. Her story celebrates in words and pictures the splendor of romantic love, emphasizing in the simplicity of Romeo and Juliet's story and in the simplicity of their portraits the purity of their emotional relationship. The complexity of the world and backdrop against which they are forced to act may be more difficult to understand and appreciate, but it never loses its aesthetic appeal.

Picturing the Stage

One of the barriers between modern students and Shakespeare's plays is an unfamiliarity with the theatrical conditions of the sixteenth and seventeenth centuries. Many modern students have very little experience with live theater. Although virtually every community provides high school dramatic productions and community theater events, and professional companies either make a home in or travel to all but the most remote areas of the country, many students have rarely or never attended a play. They are not at ease with modern dramatic traditions, let alone those of Shakespeare. They cannot envision the startling and tremendous transformation that occurs as unimposing lines of print become a three-dimensional, sensually rich, dramatic experience.

Picture books are particularly good at providing a temporary bridge over this gap—a bridge hopefully to be eventually replaced by trips to actual performances. *Shakespeare and Macbeth: The Story Behind the Play* (1994) by Stewart Ross, illustrated by Tony Karpinski, helps students appreciate the dramatic force of *Macbeth* by nesting a brief prose version of the tale in a fact-based story about Shakespeare's creation of the play. The text introduces readers to Shakespeare and the Globe as one theatrical season winds down and the company searches for new materials to further entice audiences. Ross quickly propels readers through a reasonable reconstruction of the writing process Shakespeare may have employed; he introduces them to the historical accounts of King Macbeth available to Shakespeare and highlights the changes Shakespeare elected to enhance the suspense and emotional force of his play. Briefly, Ross acquaints readers with some of the experiences actors in the early seventeenth century would have had during the production of a play and some of the experiences audience members would have undergone as they flocked to the Globe. A very fine, two-page, cut-away illustration of the Globe enables readers to consider in great detail how very different the experience of watching a play might be as a groundling pressed against the edge of the stage or as a wealthy merchant seated in the third-tier of the galleries virtually behind the stage. Audiences of Ross' illustrated version of *Macbeth* may not only understand the excitement of the play better than students who read only the text, but they may come away with an understanding of how the interactive environment of Renaissance public stages excited audiences.

Amanda Lewis and Tim Wynne-Jones' amazingly comprehensive *Rosie Backstage* (1994), illustrated by Bill Slavin, also uses the stage as a platform for provoking readers' curiosity about Shakespeare. Rosie's tale is set in Stratford, Canada, home of an extraordinarily fine repertory theater company specializing in Shakespeare. Rosie's mother works as a props mistress, and Rosie works at staying out of trouble, without notable success. Lewis and Wynne-Jones intersperse Rosie's adventures backstage, understage, and onstage with a fantastic tour of the multifaceted work of a professional theater company. The artistry and effort of the behind-the-scenes staff receives just as much attention as the work of the actors. New and experienced theater lovers will enjoy practicing irresistible tongue-twisters with the actors during vocal warmups and learning about the pasteboard riches of the costume warehouse and the prop department's seemingly magical Vacuform machine pumping out everything from armored breastplates to roast pigs. Rosie also learns about the traditional superstitions and ritual protections of the actors when she makes the mistake of calling the play *Macbeth* by name. But all the precautions the theater people teach her don't ward off the ghost of Will Shakespeare himself, who takes a special interest in helping Rosie learn how to navigate both the Festival stage in Stratford and the Globe in London. Rosie's adventures take place during rehearsals for *The Tempest, Macbeth,* and *As You Like It,* providing readers with the additional bonus of a casual introduction to these three plays.

Older students may initially resist reading a picture book like *Rosie Backstage,* but at almost one hundred pages, nearly evenly divided between text and illustrations, Lewis and Wynne-Jones' book is clearly neither an ordinary nor a simple tale. As an introduction to both the modern and the traditional conventions of Shakespearean productions, this colorful, fast-paced volume has no rivals.

Shakespeare in the Drugstore

Comic books and Shakespeare's plays generally do not get to inhabit the same sentence, but thanks to Workman Publishing, there is an exception even to this rule. Three of Shakespeare's plays have been produced as full-text comic books. Hundreds of colorful panels bring a visual interpretation to every line of these plays. Ian Pollock's *King Lear* (1984) stands far above the other two titles in the series. Pollock's characters are highly stylized, almost abstract in design. The backgrounds against which he sets the story are spare and modern, which makes it simple for readers to keep track of the play's many characters and complex actions. Oscar Zarate's *Othello* (1983) revels in rich, bright colors. Zarate's use of visual effects, like a maze setting for Iago's first temptation of Othello, reinforces the plot. Von's *Macbeth* (1982) is the least artistically satisfying of the trio. His renderings of characters, especially facial expressions and detail, are rough and ill proportioned. He also chooses to make Hecate African, a detail not demanded by the text. Although color-blind casting has added much to Shakespearean productions in recent years, using a dark-skinned figure only for one of the play's demonic villains seems more likely to reinforce negative racial stereotypes than to open a reader's eyes to the wonderful variety of ways these roles can be interpreted.

One of the advantages of these full-text comic books is their ability to clarify dialogue. Readers of Shakespeare's plays frequently complain about the difficulty of keeping track of characters. Most readers skim, or skip over entirely, speech prefixes, stage directions, and other pieces of textual information intended to show relationships among characters. Instead, readers focus on the column of verse parading down the center of the page. The fact that many editions of Shakespeare abbreviate speech prefixes so that Macbeth ends up being MACB and Macduff becomes MACD only heightens confusion. The Workman Publishing texts help solve these problems by putting a face with every line. Readers come away from these versions of the plays with a much fuller sense of how the different characters interact. They may still have trouble naming the characters because these version don't have speech prefixes, and in Shakespeare full names are spoken in dialogue only infrequently, but their grasp of the story and the human dynamics will likely be much clearer.

Full-text comics provide a terrific compromise for readers (or teachers) skeptical about abridgements or prose adaptations but who still desire tools for interpreting Shakespeare's dramas. They also serve as sly temptations. Many student readers can carry home a paperback edition of *Macbeth* without feeling the slightest impulse to peek at the pages. These slick comic-book versions virtually beg to be opened.

The Animated Tales

Picture books are not the only small-scale approach to visually enhancing adaptations of Shakespeare for younger readers. Anyone familiar with children's television programming will probably be able to recall a cartoon parody of a Shakespeare play. Everyone from Bugs Bunny to the Simpsons seems to indulge in a bit of Shakespeare schtik from time to time. In recent years *Wishbone,* a half-hour program that follows the adventures of a small, spotted dog as he finds himself catapulted into a variety of literary classics, has produced episodes based on *The Tempest* and *Romeo and Juliet.* More significant in scope, ambition, and artistic merit, however, is the six-part series produced by Shakespeare Animated Films Limited and Random House (1992–1993). These six half-hour films have been shown on HBO and are available for purchase through various educational companies.

The six-part series employs different artists and various styles of dramatization including animation, Claymation, and puppetry to bring *A Midsummer Night's Dream, Romeo and Juliet, Hamlet, Twelfth Night, Macbeth,* and *The Tempest* to life. Consequently, the series cannot be judged by any one of its products; each half-hour film is quite distinct from the others in the series. The muted tones and elongated forms of the characters and settings in the series' version of *Hamlet* enhance a somber and ghostly interpretation of the film. On the other hand, the colorful and fanciful puppets of *The Tempest* reinforce the fairy tale elements of the play rather than the human emotions of the conflicts.

Each of the films does, however, preserve Shakespeare's verse, choosing to make radical cuts in the quantity of his language presented to the audience rather than rewriting the poetry or simplifying it. Unlike most picture book editions, however, these films maintain more of the original violence and sexuality of the plays, suggesting that they are intended for audiences mature enough to be introduced to the original plays. These are deeply abbreviated versions of the plays rather than simplified or bowdlerized ones. Although by no means as significant as a full-scale theatrical production of a Shakespeare play, the short length and easy availability of these thirty-minute productions could easily make them a helpful visual supplement to a study of the plays.

Additional Picture Books:
An Annotated Bibliography

New picture books about Shakespeare and his plays appear annually. The decisions made by authors and illustrators about what to cut, what to keep, and what to illustrate can provide provocative material for discussion, especially among people who have read the original plays or who are comparing several illustrated versions of a single play. The list below simply represents a few more recent versions to provide a jumping off spot for teachers or students interested in examining the interpretation of Shakespeare in picture books.

Aliki. 1999. *William Shakespeare and the Globe.* New York: Harper-Collins.

A well-designed introduction to Shakespeare and his theater. Discussions of the two Renaissance Globe theaters and the recently constructed New Globe bring readers into today's vibrant Shakespeare community.

Burdett, L. 1995. *A Child's Portrait of Shakespeare.* Windsor, Ontario: Black Moss Press.

———1996. *Macbeth for Kids.* Windsor, Ontario: Black Moss Press.

———1997. *A Midsummer Night's Dream for Kids.* Windsor, Ontario: Firefly Books.

———1998. *Romeo and Juliet for Kids.* Windsor, Ontario: Firefly Books.

———1999. *The Tempest for Kids.* Windsor, Ontario: Firefly Books.

———1994. *Twelfth Night for Kids.* Windsor, Ontario: Black Moss Press.

Burdett's simplified retellings in rhymed couplets of Shakespeare's plays work as models for educators interested in studying Shakespeare with early elementary-aged children. Colorful illustrations and imaginary love letters, all authored by Burdett's students, complement the text. These volumes are not for purists but do demonstrate ways to make Shakespeare entertaining and approachable years before "Shakesfear" sets in.

Coville, B. 1997. *Macbeth.* Illus. Gary Kelley. New York: Penguin Books.

———1996. *A Midsummer Night's Dream.* Illus. by Dennis Nolan. New York: Penguin Books.

———1999. *Romeo and Juliet.* Illus. Dennis Nolan. New York: Penguin Books.

———1994. *The Tempest.* Illus. Ruth Sanderson. New York: Bantam Doubleday Dell.

Coville's retellings of Shakespeare's plays emphasize the elements of fairy tale and adventure, untangling or eliminating complex chronologies and narrative twists. The colorful and moody illustrators who enliven Coville's versions tend to represent the characters very youthfully. Coville's interpretations make fine read-alouds, but older students may find an "interpretation" of the illustrations a more enlightening study.

Kincaid, E. 1997. *Macbeth.* Adapted by J. Escott. New Market, England: Brimax.

———1996. *A Midsummer Night's Dream.* Adapted by J. Escott. New Market, England: Brimax.

———1996. *The Tempest.* Adapted by J. Escott. New Market, England: Brimax.

Kincaid's finely detailed drawings of soldiers, sprites, and spirits with carefully posed figures and heavily shadowed features are reminiscent of graphic novels and comic books and, as such, are likely to appeal to certain young readers. Escott's adaptations of the plays make no special attempt to preserve Shakespearean language or flavor but tend to include more narrative twists and subplots than other illustrated editions.

Langley, A. 1999. *Shakespeare's Theatre.* Illus. by J. Everett. Oxford: Oxford University Press.

Produced to commemorate the 400th anniversary of Shakespeare's most famous theater venue, this volume examines the two Renaissance Globe theaters and chronicles the fifteen years of design and construction necessary to create the New Globe theater.

Mulherin, J. 1989. *As You Like It.* Illus. by G. Thompson. New York: Peter Bedrick Books.

This textually dense thirty-two-page volume includes background material on the play and Shakespeare's life. Interspersed throughout the prose summary of the play are thoughtfully selected quotations. Simple, colored-pencil sketches are augmented by Renaissance woodcuts, a map, and reproductions of the play from eighteenth and nineteenth century paintings.

Stanley, D and P. Vennema. 1992. *The Bard of Avon: The Story of William Shakespeare.* Illus. by D. Stanley. New York: Morrow Junior Books.

A fine biography of Shakespeare, which nests his work within the social and theatrical traditions of his era. Carefully painted illustrations faithfully represent the architecture and dress of the era in pictures that simultaneously employ simple, clean lines and thoughtful detail. Children may enjoy the story of Shakespeare's life and success, but young adult readers will find more useful information here than most textbooks provide. One quibble: the author does not always delineate carefully enough between fact and hypothesis. For example, Shakespeare's marriage is presented as unhappy and unloving, when in fact historians know virtually nothing about his personal relationships.

Chapter Three

Shakespeare's World: Looking at the Renaissance Through Historical Fiction

One of the greatest barriers to understanding and enjoying Shakespeare's plays is our unfamiliarity with his world. Inexperienced audiences watch the antics and agonies of Shakespearean characters and wonder in amazed disbelief—What sort of people ever behaved this way? When did weird sisters wander the earth? What kind of poison did Laertes tip his blade with, and was it really legal to sell that sort of stuff? What kind of people force their thirteen-year-old daughter to get married? The conflicts and choices Shakespeare's characters face seem impossibly distant from the lives of contemporary audiences—and with good reason.

Shakespeare crafted his plays as entertainment and, perhaps, social commentary; they were never intended to mirror his society. They bear as little resemblance to the world of Elizabethan and Jacobean England as the television shows and movies we watch bear to our real world. We don't expect our homes and neighborhoods to look like those on television, where on one channel or another the wild west, a futuristic space station, and elite beach condominiums all house families, and we don't expect our parents and teachers to behave like the melodramatic, homicidal, comic, or superficial stereotypes of the characters in the media. Shakespeare's audiences recognized his settings, plots, and characters as fictional creations; we need to remember to do the same. Nonetheless, if we understand what the everyday lives and experiences of Shakespeare's audiences were, especially those of young adults, we are much more likely to understand why people found his work so exciting, and in turn, to achieve a more thorough and personal enjoyment of it ourselves.

Early Life

Historians have very few records about the experience of childhood during the sixteenth and seventeenth centuries. Children lack the resources to make such records themselves, and adults in this period had little reason to think that the typical events of childhood warranted recording. Social historians rely on diaries (Pollock, 1983); conduct books, which provided advice and lessons for both parents and children (Sommerville, 1992); and legal documents from judicial cases, coroner's inquests, and guild records (Hanawalt, 1993). Understanding childhood and adolescence in the Renaissance means, in many ways, collecting and assembling puzzle pieces—sometimes the picture turns out looking much like we might have expected, but sometimes an entirely new scene seems to come together before our eyes.

Family structure has changed some since the Renaissance, but in unexpected ways we are returning to family formations very similar to the ones Shakespeare would have known. Many Renaissance families were headed by single parents, included a stepparent, or were "blended" (Hanawalt 89). While our society encompasses many family structures due to the prevalence of divorce and single parents, in the Renaissance these variations from the traditional nuclear family were the result of early adult deaths. Shakespeare does not make family dynamics the primary subject of many of his plays, but a thoughtful reader or audience member is sure to notice the frequency of broken families in his works. To name just a few examples from some of the most familiar plays, Hamlet loses his father, and many characters have no mother in the plays, including Ophelia and Laertes in *Hamlet*, Miranda in *The Tempest*, and Cordelia and her sisters in *King Lear*. In *A Winter's Tale*, Perdita even grows up with foster parents. Although, as many feminist critics have pointed out, the frequent absence of mothers in Shakespeare's plays represents the rigidly patriarchal organization of Renaissance England, it at the same time serves as a reminder that many young adults did not live with intact biological families.

Education was, however, a very different experience for Renaissance children than it is for students today. The literacy rate was rising in England throughout the Renaissance, but schooling was still very haphazard. Boys might begin their education at a dame school (a small home school taught by a local woman) or at a grammar school. Dame schools taught little beyond the basics of reading and writing (McDonald 1996, 266). A boy's attendance depended largely on the economic well-being of his parents. Boys from families employed in agriculture often couldn't be spared from the farm more than a couple of months each year, and their parents might not be able to afford much in the way of tuition. Boys in this position might learn basic reading and mathematical skills, but never learn to write so much as their own name. Many boys never received the opportunity to attend school at all. Male children from wealthier families often continued their schooling through the age of fourteen. By the late Renaissance, anyone intending to go into trade, either in a family business or through an apprenticeship, was expected to be comfortably literate. In the wealthiest families, tutors might be employed to teach boys at home. At about fourteen years of age boys intending to enter jobs in the legal profession, government, or the church would be sent to the Inns of Court, Oxford, or Cambridge to complete their studies. Since Shakespeare's father enjoyed an important position as a town official, young William Shakespeare was entitled to attend the excellent Stratford Grammar School for free; like the vast majority of men in this period, he probably did not attend a university.

Girls received even less education than boys in the Renaissance. A few girls attended dame schools, but most schools were restricted to boys, so any education beyond basic reading and writing skills could only be attained at home. Some fathers and mothers were careful to teach their daughters at home and selected books of history, sermons, and conduct to help them "improve" their minds and souls. Girls in the upper class were also sometimes provided with tutors to further their education and to provide lessons in music and other ladylike accomplishments. Records of famous women's libraries and even, occasionally, their poetry and letters, assure us that some girls were well educated in the period, but such opportunities were provided only very infrequently.

Regardless of class or gender, however, childhood was a dangerous experience in this period. Roughly twenty-five to thirty-five percent of children died before reaching the age of fifteen. Statistics vary according to region and decade—cities were more dangerous than the country, and years with heavy epidemics saw higher rates of death than years that were spared the scourge of plague or other deadly diseases (Stone 1977, 68). Shakespeare himself experienced the tragic death of children in his family. He had six siblings, but two of his sisters died very young. Later in life Shakespeare had three children of his own, but he lost his only son, Hamnet, when the boy was eleven years old.

Looking at Country Life in *A Parcel of Patterns*

In *A Parcel of Patterns* (1983), Jill Paton Walsh recreates with terrible beauty and painful poignancy the effects of the plague upon the small village of Eyam and upon the life of sixteen-year-old Mall Percival. Although Walsh's book is set in the middle of the seventeenth century, more than forty years after Shakespeare's death, it captures with frightening accuracy several elements of the Renaissance world. Walsh recreates the daily routines and webs of social relationships among financially secure rural folk, the conflicts and doubts raised by competing interpretations of Protestant Christianity, and the grievous destruction wrought on a small community tormented for thirteen months with an epidemic of bubonic plague.

In this small gem of a novel, Mall Percival's first-person narration invites readers into the friendly and vibrant community of Eyam in Derbyshire. Mall's days are filled with domestic tasks, but she most enjoys caring for her small flock of sheep housed on the uplands above the village. These tasks are a mere hobby for Mall, who was given a pet lamb as a child and enjoys the money she earns from shearing and selling her sheep each year. On the hills each day she tends her flock and meets with Thomas Torres, a shepherd from the nearby village of Wardlow. Their quiet romance grows slowly because both young people know Mall's father, who makes his living maintaining Eyam's lead mines, scorns to marry his only child to a poor shepherd.

Like the other young women of the village, Mall enjoys gossiping about the elegant new dresses the parson's wife has ordered from the local tailor to be made from stylish patterns sent from London, wandering wide-eyed through the foundations of the new manor house being built by the local gentry, and helping her friend Eliza write a young man's name on a slip of paper and burn it as a charm to end her love for him—since he has decided to wed another girl. Mall measures time primarily through the passing of the seasons and marks events with the celebrations of the church calendar, like Twelfth Night (January 6). She helps her friend Emmot prepare the linen for her dowry and joins her at the feast to celebrate her handfasting, or engagement, to Roland Torres (cousin to Mall's own secret sweetheart). Mall's days are full; her greatest fear is that her father will learn of her love for Thomas before her mother has prepared him to accept his daughter's unexpected choice.

Mall also takes an interest in the religious controversy dividing the villagers of Eyam. The novel opens with the arrival of Parson Momphesson, who believes in the Anglican forms of religion that held precedence in England throughout Shakespeare's life. Momphesson's gentle ways encourage many of the parishioners to trust him, and the cheerful practicality of his wife, Catherine, immediately endears her to the neighborhood. Nonetheless, many folk don't know what to make of a man of God who seems to enjoy frivolity and luxury and lacks the stern solemnity that has marked religious practice in Eyam for a generation. With Momphesson's arrival, Parson Stanley, beloved by the villagers of Eyam, is replaced. Stanley's Puritan beliefs emphasize plainness and simplicity in all things, but a shift in England's government has effectively removed Puritan parsons from positions of influence. The loyalties of the villagers are torn, and while the two parsons refrain from outright hostilities, the advice one parson gives a parishioner often contradicts the wisdom offered by the other.

Mall's tale, written retrospectively, continuously reflects on the religious schism; she struggles to interpret it as a warning from God or perhaps even as an explanation for the troubles soon to strike Eyam. She wonders how Parson Momphesson can let his young daughter wear crimson silk, a wide lace collar, puffed sleeves, and a beaded sash without incurring the wrath of God. Years of Parson Stanley's teachings have instilled in her a belief that "the child was dressed in a fashion fitting for a whore" (Walsh 14). She also looks to her own behavior in her search for explanations. Mall cannot decide whether her own willingness to play with girlish love charms, like the day she and Emmot hide a sixpence in the Bible and wait for a dream of their future husbands' faces, is harmless fun or a heathenish sin. As the plague spreads and intensifies, Mall's confidence and ability to make sense of the world around her disintegrates.

The effects of the plague on Eyam village can hardly be overestimated. When the book opens in 1665, more than four hundred people live in Eyam; by the time the plague has passed, the names of 267 victims march in line down the pages of the parson's record book. The villagers trace the beginning of the epidemic to the death of the tailor, who falls ill only hours after unwrapping the dress patterns sent from London for Catherine Momphesson's new gown. The first death fails to alarm anyone, since sicknesses were a common trial in this period; as Mall explains, every season brings its own illnesses—from foul water, foul meats, winter chills, or summer heat. But the plague brings special sufferings:

> Most often the stricken persons would feel ill and fevered, and betake themselves to bed. There in a day or two, they would be afflicted with swellings of horrible size. The swellings arose in the groin of the sufferer, or in the side of the neck, so that the head was twisted over to one side, or in the armpit or, in some few, in the elbow. The swellings were tight and red and hard, and horrible sore. Sometimes

the swellings would burst open and give forth a foul and stinking effusion, and if they did so then there was hope for the poor sufferer. But if the tumors broke not the fever would become worse, and the victim would bleed easily from the nose, and at last would be covered with blotches, the ill-famed plague-tokens, which were livid red marks upon their bodies like great blood-blisters beneath the skin. If the tokens were once seen, hope was there none of recovery. (Walsh 54–55)

Soon the spread of the disease begins to unravel the very fibers that knit the small community together. In desperation, people seek help from any remedy they hear rumored. Some try writing the name of St. Roche on a piece of paper and eating it. Some try drinking melted bacon fat. Others simply look for ways to place blame. One embittered village woman ponders each new death and decides what sins the victim has been punished for; her self-satisfied declarations infuriate grieving family members, but clearly she finds relief in the knowledge that her own shortcomings are not the kind that bring such retribution.

Walsh details even more carefully the small medical remedies available to the people of this era. Mall helps the overworked Goody Trickett prepare herbal infusions, and the author uses these scenes to show readers both the state of the medical arts in the seventeenth century and the difficulty and danger poor, unschooled women could fall into through practicing them. While many were grateful for even the small comforts these herbal broths provided, others saw them as a way of interfering with God's plans and labeled them witchcraft.

The gradual depletion of the village's population leads to terrible compromises. Poor Robert Wood, realizing the two orphan children he lives with won't be able to help him, digs his own grave, lines it with straw, lies down in it, and waits two days in the ground for death to take him. Parson Stanley counsels the villagers to remember the duties of Christian charity and to minister to their neighbors in need. He believes God's will cannot be avoided or escaped. Parson Momphesson preaches that God helps those who help themselves; he tells the parishioners to avoid contact with the infected and to leave their nursing to him. Mall doesn't know whom to believe, but fears to meet with her sweetheart, Thomas, on the hills for danger of infecting him; the death of her father removes the one obstacle her love faced, but only strengthens her resolve to stay away from Thomas until the plague passes.

Mall's central conflict, the decision whether to seek comfort from the grief and pain of the plague with Thomas or to protect him by refusing to see him, is mirrored in the Oath of Eyam. Several months into the epidemic some villagers begin to leave. Recognizing that these people will only carry the plague with them and bring grief to other communities, Parson Momphesson convinces the village to impose a quarantine upon themselves:

> We will confine ourselves utterly within the parish bounds. And so I will promise the Duke. None shall cross the parish bounds, for life or death, until the Plague has run its course and departed from us . . . we will use the boundary-stone to leave notes of requisition for all we have need of, and the Duke will send us those things. His messengers will leave goods early in the morning, and we not come to take them till mid-day. (Walsh 91)

To many of the villagers Momphesson's plan sounds like little more than a death sentence, but when Parson Stanley adds his support to his former rival's plan, explaining that God will strike those He seeks in Eyam or wherever else they may hide, every villager swears an oath upon the Bible either to Momphesson or Stanley, as befits their religious preference. The reconciliation of the two parsons is ultimately much more horrifying than their division because it speaks so painfully and so poignantly of the community's sufferings.

The vow, no doubt, protects many of Eyam's neighbors, but for Mall it brings only bitter ironies. Her friend Emmot, who had risked her fiancé's death by visiting with him, eventually succumbs to the plague without transmitting it to him, while Mall, who knows how desperate Thomas is to break the quarantine and see her, sends a false report of her death to him to ensure he stays away from the village. In despair and unwilling to live without her, Thomas enters Eyam and offers himself as a gravedigger. To his joy he finds Mall still among the living, though both her parents are dead. A quick wedding is arranged, and they live in happiness for only a few weeks before Thomas falls ill and dies. Breaking the quarantine didn't hurt Emmot, but maintaining it nearly destroys Mall. Her grief transforms into depression even after the plague ends and the quarantine is lifted. Finally, reminded of a charm she practiced in her girlhood, Mall seeks to free herself of grief by writing her tale down so she can leave it behind her.

The most powerful elements of this tale come from the author's concluding note. Although the characters are fictional, the story of Eyam's self-imposed quarantine and devastation by the plague of 1665–1666 is a matter of historical record. Readers of Walsh's small but moving novel cannot help but develop a strong sense of the terror and suffering the plague brought to the people of the Renaissance. The plague was, of course, not limited to small rural villages like Eyam; in fact it wrought even more terrible ravages upon the city of London. During the period from December 1592 to 1593 (when Shakespeare was twenty-eight to twenty-nine years old), almost 11,000 people died in London. The size of this epidemic led to the closing of the theaters. Although the medical professionals of the Renaissance were not exactly sure how the plague spread, they did recognize that large gatherings of people seemed to aggravate the epidemic. Therefore, they kept records of plague deaths, and when the disease began to kill more than forty people a week (the number varied a bit from year to year), the authorities prohibited public gatherings—including performances at theaters like the Globe (McDonald 20). Some years the plague spared London. Some years the theaters were closed nearly as much as they were open. Surviving records do not tell us what Shakespeare did during these enforced vacations. Perhaps he stayed in London writing new plays; perhaps he returned to his wife and family in Stratford to escape the contagion. We do know from other social records, however, that people with the financial resources to abandon the city and take up residence in the country often sought such remedies when the plague grew too threatening. Some theater companies packed up a few wagons with props and supplies and used the time to tour the cities outside of London.

The Roaming Life of Actors
in *A Little Lower Than the Angels*

Shakespeare himself grew up in a period in which the world of theater was changing dramatically. For many years entertainers had wandered the English countryside, putting on performances whenever they could gather an audience. Some of these minstrels, jugglers, and players probably specialized in physical comedy and acrobatic feats, others performed verse plays, which may have originated as holiday entertainments at England's universities and law schools, and still others probably trafficked in the traditional morality plays and Mystery Plays.

Mystery Plays were by definition spiritual dramas. The central "mystery" in all of them was the salvation of mankind through the redemption of Jesus Christ. Traditionally, each Mystery Play used an event or episode from the Bible as a sort of symbol or prophecy of the deliverance of humanity. The plays were usually arranged in cycles—sometimes containing as many as forty-eight short plays—that moved from the Creation through the Last Judgment, though different local communities had different numbers of plays and featured different episodes from the Bible. Mystery Plays were most typically performed during the early summer religious festivals called Whitsuntide and Corpus Christi. In most communities each of the individual plays would belong to a guild or civic organization. For instance, the Shipwrights might be responsible for the Noah's Ark Mystery, since it had such a close association with their trade. In fact, the word *mystery* comes from an older term, *mistere*, which means trade or craft. During the festival, each play would be performed in sequence with a large percentage of the community taking part in at least one play. Since these plays were generally passed down through oral tradition and were lost when they went out of fashion, only four sets, or cycles, of them are still in existence today. During Shakespeare's childhood, Mysteries may have been among the sorts of performances put on by traveling actors visiting Stratford-upon-Avon. The productions of traveling performers were virtually the only sort of exposure to plays Shakespeare could have enjoyed during his childhood. At this time there were no theaters in England.

Geraldine McCaughrean's *A Little Lower Than the Angels* (1987) captures the world of a troop of traveling performers. The exact chronological setting of the novel is never specified, but internal events suggest that it takes place sometime after 1348 when the Black Death first reached England and before 1534 when King Henry VIII declared himself Head of the English Church and dissolved the British monasteries. Fortunately, an exact date isn't important, for there is little reason to believe that the life of a traveling performer would have changed much between the late Middle Ages and the years of Shakespeare's childhood.

The novel opens as young Gabriel slips from his perch high along the stone walls of a church where he has been assigned to work on the masonry. His tools crash to the ground below nearly injuring his master. Gabriel, it soon appears, is not well suited for a life of stone work. Colley the Mason accepted him as an apprentice only for the sake of the money his parents offered. At eleven, Gabriel is young to have been bonded as an apprentice; with his slight build he is unable to manage the heavy tools of the trade. His tears and his unabashed homesickness only serve to further anger his master and emphasize his unsuitability as a stone mason.

When work in the church is interrupted by the performance of a Mystery play acted by a traveling troop of entertainers, Gabriel watches with astonishment. Never having seen a play before, or even heard of one, he believes he has seen God and the Devil appearing before his very eyes. When "God" himself asks Gabriel if he would like to join the company as an angel, the boy is not even sure how to answer the question morally. Gabriel feels shame for breaking his apprentice bond, but he cannot imagine refusing "God" either. His confusion furthers when the "Devil," known in the company as Lucie, gives him a careful list of instructions to follow if he wants to be accepted into the troop. Not only does Gabriel understand very little of what he is being told, he can hardly bring himself to obey a man who walks like a wolf, who grins from a face dark with vile green paint, and who casually throws men into the

Hell Mouth constructed atop the pageant wagon. But the "Devil's" words don't sound evil:

> We need to be liked. We need to be respectable. One grain of trouble
> would gall the clergy and the councillors like a pin under a saddle.
> We're pioneers, boy, breaking new ground—planting new footprints
> on God's old Earth. There's none like us. Instead of plays being acted
> by the city craftsmen once a year, we've made a craft of play-acting.
> It's our profession. (15)

Gabriel's confusion of actors with roles only deepens as his success playing an angel in the company's productions grows. He does not understand why he has been chosen for the honor of an angel, but the increasing comfort of his life in terms of food, warm clothing, and friendly relationships seems, to Gabriel, to confirm his position as one of God's chosen. Gabriel's naivete amuses many of the adults in the troop, but the leader of the company refuses to let anyone disabuse him of his notions. The leader, Garvey, himself takes the role of God in the productions, and he enjoys and manipulates Gabriel's blind devotion and loyalty.

Not every town the actors visit welcomes them. Stopping to get permission from the Bishop of Greathaven before they begin their performance, the company is insulted by a clerk:

> "Morris dancers and mudwater-medicine merchants!" mouthed the
> Bishop's secretary, jabbing his eyeglasses in the playmaster's face . . . .
> "No script? No scholars? You shouldn't be allowed to represent the
> Bible and God's holy saints. And you won't in this town. I won't so
> much as put your petition in front of my Bishop. I wouldn't waste his
> time on you. He's a busy man. Away with you and your mumming!"
> (24–25)

Instead of moving on, however, the company succumbs to temptation. Garvey knows that a town full of people denied entertainers will surely be all the more hungry for some fun. If they put on a play in Greathaven, even without sanction from the Bishop, their profits should be unusually high. Halfway through their performance, they are discovered and interrupted by the Bishop himself; he orders the actors locked up for the night as vagrants. And in their absence, the pageant wagon is looted and burned by the local citizens who are quite as willing to entertain themselves with destroying the actors' art as they are with applauding it.

Without their props and equipment, the company cannot produce much in the way of spectacle and glamour to entice an audience. So, Garvey turns to a different form of marvel to please the audiences. He plants a "blind man" in the audience who, after hearing Gabriel's performance as an angel, suddenly finds his sight "restored." No one is more

amazed at this miracle than Gabriel; his astonishment and faith in the
wondrous event only serves to facilitate the ruse:

> Sometimes a woman knotted up with arthritis like a ship's ropes
> would throw up her gnarled hands and swear that her pain was gone.
> A young woman with her hands clapped over her head would say that
> her headache had flown away on wings, like a butterfly. An old man
> with only one eye said that he saw the Virgin Mary standing behind
> Gabriel, dressed in purple and green. The lame walked. The deaf
> heard. The dumb spoke. (47–48)

Soon news of the actors with their miraculous angel spreads. Crowds
gather wherever they go, petitions and valuable offerings are left on the
wagon by the gullible and desperate. Lucie's disgust with the performances grows ever more apparent; for Gabriel this is only evidence that
the man really is the Devil. His confidence in the miracles only begins
to dissolve when Lucie's daughter, Izzie, explains to them why they
don't leave the company:

> To save the Words, of course. The words of the plays. They were passed
> down father-to-son from Father's great-great-grandfather to him, and
> every one of them acted on the pageants, father and son. Now the
> plays are dying and Father's got the memory of them locked up in his
> head and no one to pass them to. No son, you see. Only me. Girls can't
> play on the Pageants. Girls can't play any kind of play. (56)

Gradually the evidence accumulates; a priest attacks the members of
the company as sinners, Garvey threatens him when Gabriel suggests
he might soon be ready to retire, a Lord tosses them out as charlatans,
and Colley the stone mason recognizes his old apprentice and insists on
joining the company for a cut of the profits himself. God may work in
mysterious ways, but these turns of events finally convince Gabriel that
something other than God is at work in the company. At last the troop
finds itself inadvertently performing at the manor house of a plague-
infected village. When the performance brings no relief from their sufferings, the maddened victims attack the company destroying the props,
scattering the members. Everything that remains has to be burned.

Gabriel spends a quiet winter with Lucie, Izzie, and a few of the
more dedicated performers gradually building a modest, but more traditional, pageant wagon. In the spring he brings Lucie his greatest gift,
a young friar who is willing to commit all the words of the pageants
stored for so long in Lucie's memory to paper—to make them immor-
tal. With the burden of carrying on the oral tradition of the pageants
lifted from him, Lucie regains the energy to lead the new little company of actors in the honest, if somewhat provincial, profession of performing plays.

Peopling her story with both dedicated artists and equally dedicated con-artists, McCaughrean captures the ambiguous status and behavior of the troops of traveling actors who provided entertainment in Britain until the end of the sixteenth century. Lucie's concern with the words of the pageants and his need for a dedicated heir to pass them on to also highlights the importance of the oral tradition in the early centuries of English theater. Shakespeare himself lived on the cusp of these traditions—in his early years he may have enjoyed the performances put on by the last generation of roving actors; during his own adulthood, he helped create the Golden Age of England's established theater culture.

Or, more accurately, in 1567 when Shakespeare was just an infant, John Brayne made the first attempt to construct a theater by building a stage and some tiers of seats in the yard of an inn called the Red Lion just outside of London. His venture does not appear to have been very successful; among other problems, he probably was unable to predict when traveling companies would be available to perform or what quality of entertainment they would offer. Nonetheless, his project was visionary and would soon serve as a model for other entrepreneurs.

The impetus for building these first real theaters came in 1572 when the Act for the Punishment of Vagabonds went into effect. This law was part of a series of official attempts to limit the number of beggars, petty criminals, and adventure seekers wandering about the countryside. The law stated that any person without land, a master, or an established profession (especially fencers, bear wardens, players, jugglers, and minstrels) would not be allowed to wander abroad without permission from two justices of the peace. Some traveling troops of entertainers were able to find sponsors and continue their trade. These companies took the name of their patron and were known by names like Leicester's Men, the Admiral's Men, and Lord Strange's Men. Many less fortunate performers were forced to find more reliable and respectable jobs. In short, the new law forced actors to become more organized and professional at the same time as it seems to have reduced the number of entertainers.

In 1576 James Burbage built the first theater in a suburb of London and named it the Theatre. Soon other entrepreneurs followed building the Curtain, the Red Bull, the Fortune, the Swan, the Rose, and various others. James Burbage showed his business talents again in 1599 after his lease on the land for the Theater expired, and he built a new performance space, naming it the Globe.

We don't know what kinds of performances Shakespeare saw as a child growing up in Stratford or whether he ever traveled to London in his early teens and saw a play in one of the brand new theaters. We do know that by the time he made his way to London as a young man, probably in the late 1580s, that the business of theater was just beginning to flourish. The plays he wrote helped establish the art form that many people today see as the greatest literary treasure of the English Renaissance.

The City

With nearly 200,000 residents, London was by far the largest city in England during the Renaissance and the heart of the theater world. Troops of actors toured smaller towns and villages from time to time, especially when bouts of plague forced the closure of all the theaters in London, but few people outside of London had much of a chance to develop a real love or appreciation of theater. Some historians estimate that as many as half the residents of England came to London at some point during their lives. Many of these visitors came on short trips; others came for extended stays or even aspired to become permanent residents. Young people who made these longer journeys to the city usually came as apprentices or servants, and although their tasks were supposed to keep them busy from dawn to dusk, they still found time to visit the theaters of London. Without the enthusiastic support of these working class people, Shakespeare's theater would never have been able to thrive.

Servants

During the sixteenth and seventeenth centuries families tended to be larger rather than smaller. Most people made their living in agriculture, where extra hands were always needed. Children grew up helping with tasks ranging from harvesting to sheepshearing and from cheese making to spinning. Yet, most of a family's children would eventually need to find other work. The small family farms could only maintain one household, and due to England's tradition of primogeniture, the oldest son could expect to inherit the property. As they reached their teens, many children from these large families or from families with no substantial property at all went into service.

Taking service was not a demeaning job or even a lower class one in the Renaissance. All but the poorest households employed some help from time to time. Wealthier families hired several servants and generally provided bed and board for them as well. Even families from the upper-middle classes often sent their older children away to spend time in service in the home of a more established tradesman or the nobility.

Service was often the first step towards independence for the young adults of the Renaissance. Although the demands of the job could be very high, usually working from sun up to sun down, service often provided the opportunity to leave, at least temporarily, a small farm or town, see new sights, and make friends. While in service a young man or woman might make connections and discover opportunities for future employment or learn a wider range of domestic or trade skills. Most importantly, working as a servant enabled young adults to accumulate savings. Young men would use their savings to purchase an apprenticeship for themselves, to set up trade, build a home, or wed. Young women, especially those from poorer families, saved their wages for a dowry. The more money a young woman could bring to a marriage, the wider range of marital opportunities she was likely to have. Service contracts could range from a few weeks to a few years and could be renewed as often as both parties desired. After several years of service, most young people moved on to more independent forms of employment or marriage.

According to English law, children could begin service as young as seven, but few families were willing to part with their children so quickly, and most employers found pre-adolescents too unreliable and too unskilled to be useful additions to their households (Hanawalt 173). Most people took service in their late teens and early twenties. Frequently, if a young person found a good employer and developed strong relationships with him, younger brothers and sisters would be sent successively to work in the house as older siblings completed their service. This kind of trust between an employer and the people who worked for him was especially important for young women. As much as they needed the wages earned by working as a servant, many young women feared sexual assault from their employer or other men in the household. The patriarchal system of authority, which organized English government and households, made it very difficult for young women to refuse the demands of a male employer, even if he were to make immoral demands and ask for sexual favors. Young women in such a position were forced to choose between losing their good reputation and losing their position. Records of servant girls being evicted by angry wives and legal cases involving servants suing for financial support for their bastard children from former employers indicate that such predicaments were far from uncommon. Similarly, boys in service were also in danger of sexual abuse from their master or older men in the household (Jardine 69–70). Service could provide significant opportunities for young adults, but it was important to choose an employer carefully; the recommendation of a good family friend or a cheerfully employed older sibling was probably worth a lot more than an extra shilling or two from an unknown employer who might try to take sexual advantage of employees, beat them, or cheat them of their wages.

Looking at Service in *The Shakespeare Stealer*

Editorial scholars of Shakespeare are quick to point out that the plays we read and watch have been through many hands since the Bard first composed them. It is very difficult, in some cases impossible, to tell any longer what is "original" in a play and what is a later addition or correction. We know that some of Shakespeare's plays were printed from his *foul papers*—a version similar to a rough draft. Other plays were printed from *the book of the play*—the copy used by the actors during performances, which might have included notes about entrances and exits, cuts or additions added in rehearsal to improve the production, and lists of props or special effects. Some plays may even have been printed from *memorial reconstructions*. In these instances actors, who had probably left the company, sat down and wrote out from memory as much of a play as they could recall and then sold this version, which would almost certainly have been full of mistakes and omissions, to another acting company or a printer. In the fast-paced and lively novel *The Shakespeare Stealer* (1998), Gary Blackwood imagines another way that Shakespeare's plays might have changed hands.

When he is only seven years of age, the orphan Widge is put to service in the rectory with the Dr. Bright, a charlatan scholar who has developed a fictional version of shorthand, called Charactery, and who steals sermons from other local preachers rather than go to the trouble of writing his own. Although the author, Blackwood, refers to Widge as an apprentice, he seems to be misusing the term. Widge is too young technically to become an apprentice and instead of teaching him his trade, Dr. Bright merely uses Widge as an assistant. Besides, rectors and other religious officials were not one of the Renaissance professions that taught their trade through apprenticeships. Widge's life is better understood as that of a servant than an apprentice.

At fourteen Widge's life takes an abrupt turn when his services are suddenly sold to Simon Bass, a lover of both theater and profit. Bass explains to Widge that his new work will include using his skill at Charactery to secretly copy the plays of Mr. Shakespeare:

> I am a man of business, Widge, and one of my more profitable ventures is a company of players. They are not nearly so successful as the Lord Chamberlain's or the Admiral's Men, but they do a respectable business here in the Midlands. As they have no competent poet of their own, they make do with hand-me-downs, so well used as to be

threadbare. . . . Now someone, sooner or later, will pry this *Tragedy of Hamlet* from the hands of its poet, Mr. Shakespeare. . . . I would like it to be us, and I would like it to be now, while it is new enough to be a novelty. Besides, if we wait for others to obtain it, they will do a botched job, patched together from various sources, none of them reliable. (32–33)

Bass sends Widge off to London in the company of the mysterious and threatening fellow servant, Falconer. Widge's wonder at the simultaneously magnificent and dismal sights of London introduces readers to this Renaissance city with splendid authenticity. Widge trips in the open sewer, marvels at the evening curfew imposed within the city, stares at the diverse mix of classes mingling in the streets, grows seasick taking a water taxi across the Thames, and falls in love with his first theatrical performance at the Globe.

Widge's initial attempt to record the production of *Hamlet* is foiled by the magic of the stage; he becomes so wrapped up in the story that he forgets to write down what's happening. He applies himself to his new trade more diligently the second time he watches the play, but inadvertently loses his book of notes to a clever pickpocket. And by then it is too late. The more time Widge spends in the theater, the more he grows enamored of the actors and their work. When they offer to take him in as an apprentice of their own, Widge finds his loyalties painfully divided. Unsure whether to throw in his lot with the happy family of the Lord Chamberlain's Men and risk violence from Falconer and Simon Bass for failing to complete his mission or steal the book of the play from the unsuspecting actors in order to keep faith with his master, Widge decides to simply play for time.

There are no explicit historical records of acting companies taking on apprentices, nor was the art of the theater respectable enough in the sixteenth and seventeenth centuries to qualify for the formal sorts of apprenticeship regulated by the guilds. Furthermore, the theatrical apprentices in this story, whose parents are reluctant to see them in this trade, also receive a small payment for the boys' services. This version of the economic system is completely backwards. People paid, and paid very well, for the privilege of becoming an apprentice in the Renaissance. Aside from these misunderstandings of the labor market, Blackwood's imaginative re-creation of the structure of the Lord Chamberlain's acting company is very convincing. Small boys work as servants waiting hopefully for more exciting assignments. A handful of teenagers, like Widge, play small male roles moving eventually into the more demanding female roles. After adolescence has passed, these young men are offered hired positions in the company—though this transition from ingenue to hero required significant shifts in performance ability, and even self-image, and could, no doubt, be very difficult, as is illustrated by Blackwood in the character of Nick. The plight of young women who may have wished to perform but were forbidden by long-standing tradition from appearing on stage is also compassionately rendered through the character of Julian. Although historically unlikely, this character does remind modern audiences of the tremendous gaps between the opportunities available to boys and to girls in the period.

In addition to Widge's social, emotional, and moral growth as he develops from a misused and obedient servant whose world view includes the insight, "Right was what benefited you, and anything which did you harm was Wrong" (Blackwood 6), to an independent young man capable of balancing his own needs and desires against those of other people, the highlight of the novel is the rich portrait of the theatrical world of Shakespeare's London. Blackwood is obviously well versed in the social and literary history of the Renaissance stage. Not only does Mr. Shakespeare himself make fleeting and wry appearances in the book, but so too do Armin, Heminges, Sly, Burbage, Beeston, Kempe, and Jonson—all real figures from the early seventeenth century. Some, like Armin, are developed into full-fledged characters in the novel, others simply pass through. Readers new to the study of Renaissance theater will be unable to distinguish the historical figures from those of Blackwood's invention, but more sophisticated readers will enjoy the humorous interplay of the real and the imagined.

Widge's adoption into the theater company also presents Blackwood with wonderful opportunities for detailing the physical construction and interior workings of a theater. Widge learns about the dangers of the Globe's thatched roof construction when the wad from a cannon accidently lights a small fire; he experiences the rich interplay of mostly memorized lines and impromptu additions when he spends an afternoon serving as the prompter at a performance; with the other apprentices, Widge spends hours working on his fencing and stage combat skills; and he is especially awed and amazed once he is promoted to playing a fallen soldier on stage by the trick swords and hidden bladders of pig's blood, which add such gory reality to the battlefield scenes. Liberally sprinkled throughout the text are dozens of references to other Renaissance plays from *Tamburlaine* to *Twelfth Night*. Some, like *Romeo and Juliet*, will be familiar to readers; others, like Ben Jonson's *Satiromastrix*, might spur readers to further investigation. Blackwood's novel does a fine job of filling in the action and humor of live stage productions, which when joined with Shakespeare's imaginative language make Renaissance theater so compelling. Widge's fear of the mysterious Falconer and avaricious Bass, his moral dilemmas, and his growing friendship with the other young men in the company serve to create a plot as exciting as the historical setting.

The New and the Old

Susan Cooper's exciting new novel, *King of Shadows* (1999), provides another introduction to the world of Shakespeare's theater. The story begins in 1999 with young Nathan Field, who has earned the opportunity to travel with a troop of American boy actors to perform *A Midsummer Night's Dream* on the New Globe stage in London. Unfortunately, Nat falls ill, and when he wakes up, he discovers that he has inexplicably been transported back in time to 1599. His new comrades interpret his confusion about everything from toilet facilities to items of clothing as the lingering effects of a fever and his excessively prim background. They believe he is a student from the elite St. Paul's School who has been loaned to the Lord Chamberlain's Men to fill the role of Puck in a revival production of *A Midsummer Night's Dream*. Nat's emotional response to his four-hundred-year journey alternates between terror and delight. He is scared he will never find his way back to his own era, but he is thrilled to meet and work with the real Will Shakespeare.

Nat's mystification with many of the practices and habits of the Renaissance actors mirrors the confusion new scholars also feel when they attempt to understand a distant historical period. In the *Shakespeare Stealer*, Gary Blackwood uses the strategy of a country boy making his first foray into the big city to introduce readers to Renaissance London. Cooper's clever time travel strategy functions in much the same way, but also allows her to make comparisons between now and then that are likely to fascinate many readers. Nat is stunned to be offered beer with his breakfast, to sleep on a straw mattress, and to view decapitated heads perched on spikes above London Bridge. He misses the security and comforts of home. Even negotiating the smallest of everyday tasks is a challenge for Nat in 1599, but Cooper makes these small trials exciting and effectively educates readers about the ordinary life of London citizens during the Renaissance.

The differences between the New Globe and the original Globe of 1599 are also presented to readers, but Nat discovers above all else how little has changed in the life of an actor from one century to the next. Competition among the ambitious and talented is common in both eras. One young member of Shakespeare's company resents Nat's presence and skills until, acting instinctively, Nat saves his life by performing the Heimlich maneuver on him. It almost proves his undoing; no one has ever seen such a thing before, and Nat needs to draw on his improvisational skills to explain his strange knowledge. Eventually, Nat learns that in any century an acting company must work as a family to win applause, and the eager talent and commitment he shows to the profession serves him well on both stages.

Cooper reinforces the importance of families through the relationship she builds between Nat, who has lost his father, and Shakespeare, who has lost his son. In an attempt to comfort the lonely boy, Will Shakespeare copies out a sonnet as a gift to Nat and tells him,

> "I have no picture of what may become of us after we are dead, Nat," he said. "But I do know thy father's love for thee did not die with him, nor thine for him. Nor mine for my Hamnet—or for this lady. Love is love. An ever-fixed mark. Remember that, and try to be comforted." (105)

The relationship ripens as the time for the company's performance draws nearer, and Nat learns that Queen Elizabeth herself secretly intends to attend. Anticipation mingles with fear—will the Queen approve of their skills or in her disappointment destroy the company? Shakespeare takes the role of Oberon in this production of the play, and the personal relationship he and Nat enjoy heightens the emotional impact of their performance as master and servant on stage. When the command performance finally begins, every element of the production falls into place, even a few risky special effects selected expressly to flatter the Queen. Nothing pleases Nat more, however, than the fact that Will Shakespeare approves of his performance:

> Will Shakespeare reached out as he passed and grabbed my hand, holding it hard, pulling me with him, and we bowed together amongst the rest as the audience cheered and clapped. And that moment above all is what makes me say I shall never have a day like that again. (134)

Going to bed that evening Nat wonders what will become of him now that his brief employment with the Lord Chamberlain's Men has been completed, but when he awakes, Nat finds himself a patient in a modern hospital just recovering from a medically mysterious case of bubonic plague. Nat's readjustment to his own era is almost more difficult than his initial adjustment to Elizabethan England. He is frustrated with the direction and interpretation of the modern performance of *A Midsummer Night's Dream*. He longs to explain how it is "supposed" to be done, and he misses the rapport he shared on stage with Shakespeare. Finally, he confides in two members of the company, but instead of laughing at him, as Nat expects, they believe, and even help him scour theatrical records to find evidence to support his story. More importantly, they help him find a copy of the sonnet Will Shakespeare gave him, and rereading those words, Nat remembers that love is for all time, and even a span of four hundred years cannot dim the feelings and experiences he shared with his hero.

Cooper's re-creation of the social and theatrical conditions of the Renaissance sparkles with well-selected details. Her characterizations of historical figures like Shakespeare, Queen Elizabeth, Richard Burbage, and even Nathan Field rely more on imagination than historical records, but as invitations to further research and exploration, they are thoroughly inviting models.

The Real World of Male Apprentices

As amusing as Widge's and Nat's adventures are, real Renaissance apprenticeships were a serious business. Skilled laborers in crafts and trades received their practical education through the apprenticeship system—a complex arrangement of contractual agreements, responsibilities, and rights that has no good parallel in the modern world. Barbara Hanawalt's fine and very readable book, *Growing Up in Medieval London* (1993) to which I am indebted, presents an especially well-detailed discussion of the hazards and rigors of apprenticeship. Although many changes reshaped the English experience between the Medieval and Renaissance periods, religious systems and government organizations were affected much more heavily than the everyday life of ordinary citizens, especially young people. Most of Hanawalt's discussion is as enlightening for fans of the Renaissance as it is for those of the Medieval Period.

In the sixteenth and seventeenth centuries apprenticeships were arranged by friends and family members. Most young adults fortunate enough to have an opportunity to become an apprentice probably had little say in selecting the type of work they would learn to do. If a boy's father were a grocer, he would most likely be apprenticed to another grocer with the expectation that he would eventually inherit his father's business. But most apprentices did not come from the city; instead, they were the children of country cousins, family friends, and ambitious men who saved their money to buy their children a chance at a more prestigious and lucrative life—connections, in these cases, were probably more significant than aptitude or preference.

Apprenticeships began as legal agreements that required a master willing and able to take on an apprentice, a boy of about fourteen years of age, and a sponsor willing to put up some money to guarantee the boy's commitment and to serve as a go-between. In addition, a boy or his parents also had to pay any entry fees the professional guild might charge and pay any room and board costs the master might charge. Apprenticeships were a very expensive investment in a young man's future. Standard apprenticeships lasted for seven years, though longer agreements were not unusual. The twelve great guilds of London carefully regulated apprenticeships with each guild adding rules and regulations necessary to its particular trade. These major guilds included

Clothworkers, Drapers (dealers in inexpensive cloth), Fishmongers, Goldsmiths, Grocers, Haberdashers (dealers in sewing notions and small wares), Ironmongers, Mercers (merchants in expensive cloth), Merchant-Tailors, Salters (dealers in salt), Skinners, and Vintners (wine merchants) (McDonald 1996, 224).

Typically, an apprenticeship contract emphasized all the things a boy could not do during his years as an apprentice. For example, apprentices were generally prohibited from marrying without permission, drinking, gambling, dicing, gossiping about the master, fornicating, wasting the master's property, taking service with another master, and running away (Hanawalt 134–35). Many apprenticeship contracts included clauses requiring the young man to continue working for a low wage for a year or two even after the apprenticeship was over. This ensured that the master would have cheap, skilled labor at his disposal as a reward for having trained his apprentice well.

To meet his side of the bargain, the master was required to provide food, clothing, shoes, and bedding to the apprentice. He was also required to teach him his craft. A master was not supposed to put an apprentice to work at menial labor, like fetching water, that an ordinary servant might do, nor was he allowed to beat or discipline him in any way that caused the apprentice permanent injury—though the vigorous corporal punishment typical in the Renaissance was considered well within the boundaries of a master's authority (Hanawalt 135). Furthermore, a master had the right to sell his apprentice's contract to another master if he saw fit. About half the masters in London took only one apprentice at a time, while the other half might have as many as six boys working for them. Some guilds regulated which of their members could take on apprentices and how many apprentices each man could take.

A new apprenticeship meant an extraordinary change fraught with many risks for both a boy and a master. Suddenly the boy found himself leaving behind all the comforts and love of his family to live with his master. He had to fit himself in to the new social and emotional worlds of his master. He also had to begin developing the skills of his new trade, working up from the most labor intensive and tedious tasks to the finer points of the craft. Most London masters only trained a few apprentices during their working lives. A poorly chosen apprentice meant that many hours were wasted, while a talented apprentice could improve a master's reputation and income tremendously.

Becoming an apprentice meant joining a new family and beginning a lifetime profession all at once. The demands and stresses on the teenage boys who became apprentices must have been tremendous; in fact, in the sixteenth century only forty-one percent of apprentices completed their contracts (Hanawalt 138). Some apprentices found their new lives absolutely unbearable and returned home or ran away, forfeiting the money paid by parents and sponsors. Apprentices who broke their contracts were usually barred from taking new contracts, especially with masters in the same trade. The unexpected death of a master or his failure to fulfill his obligations resulted in the breach of other contracts. Frequently, apprentices left simply because they had learned enough to ply their new trade back home in one of the smaller villages or towns of England—sometimes these men were runaways, but often they simply bought out their contracts. Without completing an apprenticeship, a man could never become a member of the important London guilds, but this privilege was only really important to residents of cities.

Despite this low rate of completion, many apprentices forged deep and meaningful relationships with their masters. Many masters took apprentices because they lacked sons or had lost them to early deaths. The deep emotional desire for a successor could serve as a powerful motivation toward a successful relationship. Occasionally, an apprentice inherited his master's shop or trade upon his death, others married into the family; some young men became partners with their former masters once their apprenticeships were complete. The thriving trades of London and the power of the Guilds shows that regardless of disheartening statistics, the apprenticeship system was a successful method of training young men.

Female Apprentices

Girls entered apprenticeships at a much lower frequency than boys. None of the twelve major guilds formally accepted women into their membership, but since London laws allowed married women to trade and widows to maintain their dead husband's businesses, many women must clearly have had a good grounding in the various skills and crafts regulated by the guilds. When girls did enter apprenticeships, they tended to begin at a younger age and with far less financial outlay. They also did not serve as lengthy an apprenticeship as their male counterparts. Unlike male apprentices, their contracts usually allowed a young woman to buy out her term in order to marry. Girls were usually apprenticed to women, and their trades were seemingly limited to a small number of crafts like silk thread making, brewing, and tailoring (Hanawalt 142–43). In most other respects, however, the risks and opportunities a young woman undertook through an apprenticeship mirrored those of London's many male apprentices.

Apprenticeship in *A Boy and His Bear*

Harriet Graham's novel *A Boy and His Bear* (1994) opens with grim authenticity. In 1597 Richard Stronge dies leaving behind a wife and two children, Anne (about thirteen) and Dickon (perhaps ten). As a merchant traveling through Europe, Stronge relied on the profits of each journey to sustain his family until it was time for him to make a new trip. His unexpected death leaves his family with debts and without income. Anne, who had looked forward to a good marriage, and Dickon who excelled at and enjoyed the privileged education his father was providing for him, are wholly unprepared for the losses and changes brought on by their father's death. The most difficult of these developments comes in the shape of Master Tyndal, the butcher, who begins to call on their mother and soon offers to relieve the entire family of poverty with a proposal of marriage to Widow Stronge.

The loving and joyful household of his youth becomes a grim and silent place, but Dickon never misses his father more than the day his new stepfather announces a change in his education: "'Better the boy is apprenticed and learn an honest trade,' he said. 'All this book learning will do him little good'"(9). His complete disregard for Dickon's preferences seems harsh, nearly cruel, by modern standards, but his concern and interest for the future of a nearly grown stepson marks him as a responsible Renaissance parent. His willingness to pay the apprenticeship fees serves as evidence to Dickon not of his generosity, but of a desire to have him out of the house. Dickon cannot help but see Tyndal as a kind of villain, but Graham is careful to damn him with nothing more than a sort of remote disinterest in the feelings of the child he has undertaken to support and prepare for manhood. Master Tyndal makes use of the connections established in his own trade and apprentices Dickon to Master Nashe, a tanner. The sights and smells of the dead carcasses waiting to be treated at the tannery sicken Dickon. The six-year apprenticeship contract seems like a life sentence to the boy.

The household routines of Master Nashe are no more appealing to Dickon than his work at the tannery. Dickon, the youngest and newest of the tanner's four apprentices, finds himself stuck with tedious tasks like helping Mistress Nashe serve breakfast and cleaning out the tannery workshop each morning. Mistress Nashe's insulting habits of calling him "Carrot Head" and accusing him of laziness are a sad replacement for the affections formerly lavished on him by his mother. Dickon also fears a beating with the evil-looking cane Master Nashe keeps in the corner of the workshop, though after four months of service he has yet to see it used. One of the other apprentices, Ned, makes some efforts to befriend Dickon, but their temperaments do not easily complement each other. Dickon jealously guards the few hours of leisure granted to the apprentices every Sunday afternoon. Ned wants a companion with whom to explore London. Dickon's distaste for the tannery clashes with Ned's more conventional respect for the Master and enthusiasm for his profession.

Dickon's relief from the drudgery of tannery chores comes when Master Nashe makes use of his ability to read and write and sends him to the Bear Garden with a letter concerning an order of bear hides. Dickon undertakes the errand with enthusiasm; he is, like all London boys of the period, familiar with the sport of bear baiting, but he has never before been to the Bear Garden. During the Renaissance bear baiting was considered a disreputable entertainment suitable primarily for common folk, especially men. In fact the Bear Garden and the Globe theater were located nearly next door to each other in Southwark, just across the Thames River from the hustle and bustle of London proper. Bear baiting was a betting sport during which a bear (sometimes declawed or with broken teeth to hinder its fighting capabilities) was chained to a stake and attacked by dogs. Men might wager on how many dogs it would take to subdue the bear or whether a specific dog would survive the contest.

Dickon arrives with his letter at the same time as a new load of bears is being delivered. He is simultaneously transfixed and terrified by the roaring beasts with huge claws. Yet, he cannot help but reach out to comfort and calm a frightened bear cub after he escapes and bolts across the yard toward Dickon. The older men all admire his skill with the animal; one even seems to think it might be a kind of sorcery. But the Master of the establishment quickly spots a financial opportunity. He invites Dickon to train the cub. Dickon knows he cannot legally serve two masters, but unless the cub can be made profitable, he will be killed. Dickon agrees to visit during his free hours on Sunday afternoon to work with the cub.

In addition to his anticipation for working with the cub, Dickon's days are consumed with excitement about the annual Southwark Fair. Ned explains to Dickon that like Christmas and the Saints' Days, the masters of London are required to give a holiday to all apprentices during the fair:

> "Master Nashe will give us time off," he said, squatting down beside Dickon. "A day and a half, I shouldn't wonder. You'll come with me, won't you? It will be grand, you'll see; there are jugglers and tumblers in the streets, stalls with gingerbread, things to buy, and all manner of folk to watch. And there will be plays at all the theaters and bear baiting by the river." (47)

Two events, unfortunately, quickly sour the holiday for Dickon. As usual Mistress Nashe begins the morning by criticizing him. To his shock

Master Nashe defends him and announces to the household that next week Dickon will be promoted from running errands and cleaning to working with a knife skinning carcasses and preparing the hides—these bloody and stinking tasks horrify him. Even worse, Ned hauls him off to begin their holiday by watching a bear baiting. Dickon finds the cruelty of the sport even more shocking than he had imagined. He feels only empathy for the bear:

> One huge hound had leaped at her back again, while two more at-
> tacked her from the other side. In vain she struck out with her claws.
> There were too many of them, and where one failed another suc-
> ceeded. The blood began to flow from her head and ears in a slow
> trickle and with a roar the bear tossed her head, half-blinded now and
> trying to shake the crimson gouts from her eyes. (76)

Dickon retreats from the Bear Pit to the stables to visit the cub and recover from the brutality he has witnessed. Ned follows him laughing and jeering at his sensitivities, but for all his brave words, Ned is stunned when he sees the bear cub respond to Dickon with tame affection. To Ned, who has only seen bears chained to a post rearing and growling and lashing with knife-like claws, the only explanation for the cub's behavior is witchcraft, the devil's work. Without waiting for an explanation he flees from his fellow apprentice.

Dickon's problems quickly increase. He knows returning home to Master Nashe will mean punishment—whether the Master believes, like Ned, that he is involved in witchcraft and devilry, he will certainly be whipped for taking any kind of service at the Bear Garden. Dickon considers his options, " 'I wouldn't mind the whipping.' Dickon frowned. 'I wouldn't even care if they put me in the stocks . . . that's what they do to runaway apprentices isn't it? . . . But if I go back I will never see the bear cub again'" (101–02). But before he can decide what to do, Osric, one of the employees of the Bear Garden, spitefully locks Dickon into the bear cage with the cub. He taunts Dickon with stories of watching a young woman and her familiar, a cat, burned for witchcraft. Worse yet, he heads out to spread rumors that Dickon is another witch. Graham effectively demonstrates the speed with which mob suspicions can grow and turn with anticipation toward violence, especially after several days of celebrating during the local fair. Nonetheless, Graham is historically inaccurate in including the story of a burning witch in the novel. England reserved burnings for religious heretics; condemned witches, like many other common criminals, were executed on the gallows.

Dickon's options evaporate quickly; both he and the bear cub narrowly escape when the stable is set on fire. With the aid of two sympathetic men, one from the Bear Garden and one from the Globe, he takes what may be his only chance for survival and agrees to leave London, hidden amidst a troop of French tumblers who have been performing at the Southwark Fair.

The second half of Graham's novel is much less authentic in its settings and premises than the first half, though it is undoubtedly still an exciting tale. The representations of sixteenth century stepfamilies, apprenticeship demands, and London life are all exchanged for a more fantastical setting in rural France. Gradually, Dickon finds a place for himself amidst the family of tumblers and even learns to be of use to them by playing the flute. With Rosa, the youngest of the performers, he works to train the bear cub to dance. Unwilling to use the traditional method, which involved burning the bear's paws with hot coals to force him to lift them, the two youngsters experiment with different techniques until they finally discover a painless way to teach the bear. When spring arrives, so does the Bear Catcher, who also haunts the French woods trapping animals to sell. The Bear Catcher's attempts to capture Dickon's cub finally give the now nearly fully grown animal a chance to return the kindness Dickon has showered upon him and save the boy's life. The novel ends with a very modern celebration of independence—both Dickon and the cub are freed to follow their own paths without obligation to any Master or family. The premise that a well-educated merchant's son would be satisfied joining a troop of wandering foreign performers speaks more to modern romanticized notions of life on the road than to its realities. In short, Graham's novel offers both a thoughtful vision of the life of a sixteenth century adolescent and a conclusion embracing the values of modern adolescents.

Conclusion

None of the novels discussed in this chapter will significantly help readers in understanding the plot conflicts or character development of Shakespeare's plays, but the work that they do perform may be even more important. All of these novels encourage readers to abandon stuffy, off-putting, and staid impressions of Shakespeare's plays and the world in which they originated in favor of a lively, moving, and personal vision of the Renaissance. They create a context for reading or watching Shakespeare as informed participants and not simply as victims of the curriculum. Finally, each of these novels has literary merits apart from its treatment of theatrical or historical themes. All of them have been recognized with awards or critical lauds in the United States or Britain, and were he asked, Shakespeare himself would almost certainly applaud them too.

Chapter Four

Romeo and Juliet: Reincarnations

Romeo and Juliet may feature teenage lovers preferencing impulsivity over reason, but more than anything else its place in the school curriculum seems to stand as proof positive of educators' preferencing tradition over reason. On Monday we invite students to join a debate about conflict resolution tactics. Tuesday we assign students to begin studying those peace-loving clans, the Montagues and the Capulets. Wednesday's health class is devoted to safe sex. On Thursday we explicate the balcony scene. Friday brings a lecture on mental heath and preventing teen suicide. No wonder some young adults feel lost or confused! *Romeo and Juliet* appears in classrooms because the emotions and conflicts it explores have immediate relevance for many young adults, but the decisions and conclusions the play provides run in direct opposition to the sorts of behaviors we hope students will themselves employ. Teaching the play often means teaching against the play.

An impulsively didactic reaction to this play may be impossible to escape in an era oversaturated with newsbreaking episodes of teen violence and in which suing the teacher, the school, and the district strikes some adults as a way to solve juvenile behavior problems. In her chapter on *Romeo and Juliet* in *Adolescent Literature As a Complement to the Classics* (1993), Arthea J.S. Reed provides a list of contemporary texts to pair with Shakespeare's play, which seem designed to address the problem that, regardless of the beauty of its language or the power of its plot structure, *Romeo and Juliet* seems particularly perverse in its themes and outcomes. Reed provides suggestions of young adult novels that treat suicide, peer pressure, young love, the generation gap, and several other topics. Many of these books provide thoughtful reflections upon meaningful social issues and are worthy novels in their own right. Yet, the play itself can get lost with this approach. The means and the end twist in upon each other—Shakespeare as a vehicle for discussing death or discussions of death as a tool for understanding Shakespeare?

Nonetheless, several contemporary novelists provide new spins on this well-seasoned story, illustrating through their creative reinterpretations of the play what *Romeo and Juliet* has to offer beyond sex and violence, and in a society inundated with tragedy, these revisions offer refreshment. David Belbin's *Love Lessons* (1998) takes the unusual approach of stressing the tragic nature of precipitous romance by reimagining the story in a modern setting. Avi reminds readers of the ludicrous elements of love in *Romeo and Juliet Together (and Alive!) at Last* (1987). Anne McCaffrey emphasizes the timeless and universal appeal of the drama in her science fiction novel *The Ship Who Sang* (1969). Whereas *Romeo and Juliet* transforms the young lovers into martyrs, Geoffrey Trease expands on the idea of hunted but perceptive young protagonists in *Cue for Treason* (1940), transforming them into models for the adult community. Each of these novels includes a production of *Romeo and Juliet*. On one level this plot element enables the authors to juxtapose the culturally idealized vision of romance embodied in Shakespeare's *Romeo and Juliet* with the more mundane forms of love and affection experienced by the novel's characters in their own lives (and by analogy in the reader's life as well). At the same time, this plot technique allows authors the opportunity to play at director and describe their ideas of how *Romeo and Juliet* should be understood and performed. Readers may appreciate these fictional productions or enjoy discussing their limitations.

Romeo and Juliet in the Classroom

In *Love Lessons* (1998), David Belbin confronts the thematic challenges of *Romeo and Juliet* more directly than any of the other novelists I will examine in this chapter. The decisions Romeo and Juliet make are, within the context of the play, rash and dangerous. But we don't live within the context of the play. As our distance from the world of courtyard duels and arranged marriages grows, our emotional connection to the play begins to fray. The plight of the young lovers becomes less horrifying because it no longer seems realistic enough to threaten readers. Instead, we tend to focus on those aspects of *Romeo and Juliet* closest to modern experiences—which usually means the romantic and melodramatic aspects of the play. Belbin's novel offers a modern-day Romeo and Juliet romance—one as passionately attractive and as shockingly misguided to us as the behavior of the young Montague and Capulet lovers must have been to the citizens of Verona and the audiences of Renaissance England.

Belbin is not the first Shakespearean adapter to modernize *Romeo and Juliet*. The 1956 musical revision, *Westside Story,* by Arthur Laurents, Leonard Bernstein, Stephen Sondheim, and Jerome Robbins attempts to reinvigorate the full complexity of the lovers' tale. By introducing gang violence and ethnic friction, Laurents *et al.* hoped to illustrate both the timeless elements of the story and to rescue the romance from false sentimentality. The story of Romeo and Juliet or of Tony and Maria is sentimental, but it is also raw, barren, and tragic. Shakespeare's tale surpasses many other romantic stories, not because his characters are more appealing than others, but because the sentimentality is balanced and informed by the tragic waste and destruction of the conclusion.

Westside Story also struggles to make the Romeo and Juliet story appealing to new audiences by changing the class structure. In Shakespeare's drama the two lovers both come from elite families; they risk losing a great deal when they challenge the status quo with their forbidden love. Focusing on young, working-class men and struggling immigrants, Bernstein demonstrates, on some levels, the universality of Shakespeare's vision. Yet, setting the musical among the street children of New York also serves to suggest that the well educated or those whose lives are buffered by the security wealth brings may be safe from the misunderstandings and sudden violence that erupt between the Jets and the Sharks. Bernstein's modernization of *Romeo and Juliet* creates a more contemporary setting for the story, but reinforces the distance some readers may have from the play's events by his choice of class. Interestingly, Belbin's approach to reinterpreting the drama solves the problems of time and class by relocating the play in a school—one of the most genuinely universal backdrops of our culture.

Belbin's novel also forces readers to think harder about the ages of his protagonists and Shakespeare's than we usually do. Contrary to popular belief, the age of marriage in the English Renaissance was not very different from what it is in our own period—women typically made a first marriage at about twenty-four and men at about twenty-seven (McDonald 1996, 265). Young people from the aristocratic class, who made up no more than two percent of the population, did, however, often marry at much younger ages (Wrightson 1982, 24). Their matches tended also to be arranged; the desire to preserve economic and political power superceded any beliefs about the virtue of love between marital partners. Still, while betrothals may have been arranged for the nobility even while the participants were very young children (consent to marry could be given by anyone over the age of seven), the actual marriage was rarely performed until both partners were in their middle teens or older. A girl could not legally consummate a marriage until she reached the age of twelve, and a boy was required to be at least fourteen (Wrightson 67).

Young adults from the working classes, the vast majority of the population, generally had much greater freedom to arrange their own marriages, and they were often based on affection. Readers of *Romeo and Juliet* mistakenly assume that the youthful alliance of the two protagonists would have been considered unremarkable by Renaissance audiences. Most of the people gathered at a theater to watch *Romeo and Juliet* would have found both the precipitate union of the titular protagonists and Capulet's willingness to unite his thirteen-year-old daughter to Paris just as ill-conceived as we do. In fact, Shakespeare seems to have intended to startle his audience by deliberately emphasizing Juliet's extreme youthfulness; in one of the sources he used for the play Juliet is fifteen and in another she is seventeen (McDonald 265). To recapture the shock the original audiences must have felt as they viewed the play, Belbin peoples his novel, *Love Lessons,* with disturbingly young protagonists, especially the Juliet figure, named Rachel.

Rachel is nearly sixteen when the novel opens, and her world centers almost exclusively around school. No romance with a classmate could match the taboo nature of a Capulet's passion for a Montague, so Belbin fittingly chooses a young teacher to play Romeo to Rachel's Juliet. In his early twenties and just beginning his teaching career, Mike Steadman thinks his relationship with Emma, his live-in girlfriend, is secure. Like Romeo rejected by Rosaline, however, when Emma unexpectedly abandons him, he quickly finds consolation and exhilaration in a new and forbidden romance.

Belbin's novel is very brave; the modern characters and situations he chooses to parallel *Romeo and Juliet* successfully summon the indignation many of Shakespeare's audience members must have felt when watching the play. Readers will easily believe the breathless anticipation Rachel feels as she waits to meet Mike, but they will not be able to dismiss the inappropriateness of the romance—relationships between high school teachers and high school students are absolutely out of bounds. Concern, even anger, always balances against the sentimentality of this romance in Belbin's adaptation. Modern stage and film productions of the play tend to make Romeo and Juliet enviable; in this novel readers want to scream "No!" "Stop!" "This is idiotic!" every time Rachel and Mike exchange another heated glance. The novel is agonizing in ways that Shakespeare's play should be, but often isn't.

Belbin's setting also highlights the simultaneous titillation and threat of secrecy. Perhaps it is hard to remember how dependent *Romeo and Juliet* is upon clandestine meetings and silent collaborators; today, no one comes to the play without already knowing how it ends, so the tension of untimely discovery gets lost. Belbin's novel highlights the secrecy. Initially, Rachel and Mike feel empowered by their hidden re-lationship; they know things that other people don't, and their every interaction has a level of meaning unrecognized by anyone else in the room. Eventually, the fear of discovery adds a constant strain to the re-lationship. Rachel's refusal to confide in her mother distresses both women. Mike's decision not to share his problems with his best friend, Phil, destroys their relationship. As Phil explains: "It's not that you don't tell me about it. I mean, that's up to you. No, what hurts is you think that I'm such an idiot I won't notice what's going on" (163). Belbin's emphasis on the anxiety of the Romeo and Juliet relationship enables readers to better understand that the tragic elements of Shakespeare's play are not limited simply to the deaths.

Nonetheless, by acknowledging the truly taboo nature of the ro-mance in *Romeo and Juliet,* Belbin violates a few of our own cultural boundaries. Romances between students and instructors do occur, but we don't like to admit it—for any number of complex reasons. *Love Les-sons* explicates such a romance with care and in detail, and even though, in the end, the novel vehemently damns the relationship, many read-ers, especially adult readers, will surely disapprove of the book. As in Shakespeare's play, the relationship between Rachel and Mike is con-summated. Belbin describes the sexual nature of their attraction with honesty; the graphic details he provides are certainly less explicit than most R-rated movies and many prime time television shows, but his prose is not coy or euphemistic. A hypocritical attitude that encourages students to read about love and lust in Renaissance Italy will shy away from sanctioning a similar tale set in twentieth century England. Inter-estingly, although published by Scholastic, the novel is set in Britain and has not yet been offered in American markets. Online bookstores like the United Kingdom division of Amazon.com make it easy enough to purchase, however.

The parallels in *Love Lessons* extend beyond the Juliet–Rachel and Romeo–Mike similarities. A few of the secondary characters in Belbin's novel suggest thoughtful parallels with the supporting characters in *Romeo and Juliet.* As mentioned before, Mike's first girlfriend, Emma, serves as a kind of Rosaline. Romeo's first girlfriend never actually ap-pears on stage during Shakespeare's play. Mike's Emma doesn't fare much better. She's often absent when Mike expects to find her at home, and most of what readers learn about her comes from his recollections about their relationship. Shakespeare's Nurse also has a parallel in Bel-bin's novel. Like Juliet, Rachel tries to keep her relationship secret but discovers she needs some help. Juliet turns to her nurse and Rachel turns toward her childhood friend Becky. Initially, Rachel fears that Becky will be shocked or disapproving, but like Shakespeare's Nurse, who has a very earthy and robust attitude toward sexuality, Becky refuses to make any judgments: "Who knows what's right or wrong" she says (181). Fortunately, Becky also shares the Nurse's practicality; she forces her friend to get birth control.

Finally, Phil Hansen, Mike's colleague at the Stonywood School, fills the role of Mercutio. Phil shifts from a supportive friendship to an angry antagonism with Mike. Like Mercutio, who grows angry at Romeo's refusal to fight Tybalt, Phil feels he has risked a great deal for Mike. Phil shares his apartment with Mike after Emma leaves him, and the two men go to clubs and bars together. When he discovers that Mike is involved with a student, he fears that his own professional reputation will be tainted as well. Budget cuts eventually force the school to fire Phil, but Mike was the last staff member hired and should have been the first to be released. Just as Mercutio absorbs the angry and lethal blow Tybalt had originally meant for Romeo, Phil feels he has been unwillingly sacrificed in Mike's place.

Love Lessons explores *Romeo and Juliet* overtly as well as through the character pairings. Shakespeare's play is the assigned text for the students in the eleventh form at Stonywood (the British equivalent of an American twelfth-grade class), and to simplify matters the drama coach decides to use it for the school's spring play too. Throughout the novel characters discuss how the roles in *Romeo and Juliet* should be cast and interpreted. They also repeatedly investigate the meaning of "love":

> "Why do Romeo and Juliet fall in love so suddenly?" the teacher asked, then proceeded to answer his own question. "Some people argue that they're destined for each other. A case can also be made for their romance as youthful rebellion; subconsciously, they want to show up their elders and the stupid feud between the two families. Then there's the romantic view: love at first sight."
>
> "What about the lust theory?" Becky suggested. "They fancy each other like crazy and can't wait to start bonking?" (123)

Superficially, Becky's indecorous question only highlights her resemblance to Shakespeare's Nurse, who also enjoys infusing serious conversations with a little lecherous levity, but Becky's interpretation also reveals an astute analysis of *Romeo and Juliet*. In addition to whatever sentimental or fatalistic motivations may be attributed to the young lovers, lust is clearly part of the equation. Belbin insists upon his readers considering this aspect of the play.

Rachel wins the role of Juliet, and a talented young actor already very devoted to her, Nick Cowan, agrees to take the role of Romeo. Belbin suggests in many ways over the course of the novel that Nick is the sort of "Romeo" Rachel should be looking for. He is young and awkward, but also sincere and loyal. Early in the book Rachel enjoys a few dates with him, but their excursions aren't glamorous. They take a bus or walk. He gets carded at a movie theater. He clearly has no more sexual experience than Rachel. Nick doesn't meet her by moonlight, woo her eloquently, or offer to take her away from her schoolgirl life. *Romeo and Juliet* has taught her to expect these sorts of behaviors from a boyfriend, and unlike Nick, Mike Steadman appears as if he can live up to these misguided expectations.

Rachel may believe that Nick is unsophisticated, but Belbin strongly emphasizes to his readers that Mike's behavior is genuinely immature. Mike enjoys the company of another teacher named Sarah, except when the staff debates ethical issues. Sarah easily refutes all the hypothetical arguments excusing teacher/student romances: "Those relationships are unequal in a lot of ways: power, money and experience" (150). Everyone but Mike ends up nodding in agreement. As his relationship with Rachel intensifies he becomes more and more self-involved. Rachel's grades drop precipitously, but Mike doesn't have time to worry about them—he even lies about her work when other teachers begin to investigate the problem. Mike promises Rachel he will find a new job so that they can live together where people don't know their histories, but when an offer comes, he declines it. As outside pressure mounts, Mike revises his vision of the romance: "Rachel was too young. She had a life to lead before she started making commitments. . . . When the time came, he would break it to her gently" (229). By the time the novel ends, Mike's Romeo games seem inescapably sordid.

Growing rumors and a few disastrous miscalculations eventually force the relationship into the open. In Belbin's modern reinterpretation of *Romeo and Juliet,* career disasters ensue rather than death. Mike must leave his job, and Rachel loses her chance to go to college in the fall to study acting. Her *love lessons* with the English teacher have only taught her that *love lessens,* at least if it is the wrong kind of love. Playing at Juliet isn't just exciting and beautiful, it is also depressing and tragic.

Belbin's ultimately didactic book argues that no matter how attractive the taboo relationship between a student and teacher might seem, it is inescapably flawed. In his afterword Belbin provides information for confidential British social services to help any student who might be involved in a similarly inappropriate relationship. To be frank, the message and the astute revision of Shakespeare offered in this novel are much more striking than its literary qualities, but the fears and hypocrisies of many adult censors may prevent many students from making this judgment for themselves.

Romeo and Juliet as Comedy

Not everyone takes *Romeo and Juliet* as seriously as Belbin. In *Romeo and Juliet Together (and Alive!) at Last* (1987), Avi highlights the comic nature of awkward, young lovers. Eighth-grader Peter Saltz has fallen in love with his classmate Anabell Stackpoole. Taking his cue from Shakespeare, he attempts to express his affection in poetry:

> There once was a fair beauty named Anabell
> For whom Pete Saltz, truly, in love fell.
> But when he offered his heart,
> She jumped up with a start,
> And said, "I have to go now because I just
> heard the end-of-the-class-bell. (4)

Pete's decision to employ the illustrious limerick rather than the more sedate forms of expression offered by the sonnet or blank verse structure to pour out his heart should serve as a warning to readers that this Romeo and Juliet story will be invested with more levity than most. The awkward, ham-handedness of the rhymes and syntax ought not to be overlooked either; these students of Renaissance drama do not worship Shakespeare's verse, they torture it!

Recognizing the hopelessness of his friend's plight (and verse), Ed Sitrow decides to help his friend. Inexperienced in the ways of love himself, Ed decides to turn to Shakespeare for help. If he can organize a class production of *Romeo and Juliet* with Pete and Anabell in the lead roles, not only will they have plenty of chances to speak to each other, but they won't even have to worry about what to say—Shakespeare will do it for them. The fact that Pete is painfully shy and extraordinarily clumsy doesn't disturb Ed in the least. Anabell also makes an unlikely Juliet:

> Stackpoole's voice, which she didn't use often, was hardly more than a whisper. Her legs and arms were thin, her hands small. A narrow freckled face was partially hidden behind stringy brown hair, which she sucked on. Maybe it was her only nourishment. If she wasn't eating this hair, she was always brushing it out of her eyes to see the book she was always reading. (6)

Avi's description is amusing, but it also serves to remind readers of the awkward appearance and demeanor of genuine thirteen-year-olds—they rarely resemble the gazelle-like creatures usually selected for professional stage and film productions.

Ed's classmates eagerly agree to join him in his theatrical matchmaking adventure, except, that is, for Albert Hamilton, the class bully. Intent on stealing any available limelight for himself, Hamilton nearly succeeds in winning the role of Romeo, but eventually settles for Tybalt—an aggressive, posturing character with whom he clearly shares more characteristics.

Like the adults in Romeo and Juliet's world, the teachers and administrators of South Orange River School have trouble resisting the urge to tinker with the lives of young people. Ed finally realizes that the best way to deter them from interfering with the production is to tell them what they want to hear. Just as Juliet agrees to marry Paris in order to deflect her parents' attention, Ed makes up misleading stories about his classmates' interest in literature and desire to demonstrate their maturity in order to gratify the suspicious educators. Mrs. Bacon, the English teacher, with her floral dresses and bustling behavior, turns out to be the most difficult to dismiss. Like Juliet's good-natured Nurse, she wants to be in on the action, even if she doesn't quite know how to help. But, like Romeo, Ed soon charms her into supporting the young people:

> "How's it going?" she'd say.
> "Fine," we'd always answer.
> "Looks good," she'd say, not that she saw anything. "Call on me when you need help," she'd add. Tipping me a wink of understanding, she'd leave. (69)

Mr. Sullivan, the school principal, serves as Prince Escalus, and like Shakespeare's character, Mr. Sullivan fails to realize just what his subjects are up to until it is too late.

On the day of the performance, nothing goes as planned. Ed places too much trust in his assistant producers, especially the costume designer. One actor looks like a Shriner and the next appears wearing armor recycled from a Tinwood Man's outfit; another player soon follows carrying a space helmet. Other characters have been costumed a little bit too literally—the Nurse wears a cap with a red cross and carries a stethoscope. Lights flicker, sets fall, props malfunction, and actors forget their lines. Albert Hamilton, however, creates the biggest problems. Denied the leading role, he decides that in this production Tybalt should win the duel between himself and Romeo. A full-fledged brawl erupts on stage; fortunately, the enthusiastic audience simply assumes it is all part of the play. Ed hastily cuts the lights and scurries out to rescue Romeo.

The performance ends with a bang. Hiding beneath Juliet's tomb (a cloth draped table), Albert lights a firecracker just as Pete leans over to kiss his beloved Anabell. In this version of *Romeo and Juliet,* however, real justice is done. The production's hot-headed Tybalt, who instigated all of the fights both in the script and in the classroom, gets hauled off by the authorities and banished from the scene with a one-week suspension when Mr. Sullivan, an unwitting Prince Escalus, hustles up to the stage to reinstate order. Avi doesn't tell his readers whether Pete and Anabell find true love once they remove their costumes and return to their daily existence as eighth graders, but by the end of the novel Ed discovers a little romance of his own—maybe he'll even take on a production of *Antony and Cleopatra* next. Avi's novel has a lot to offer readers; it is clever, amusing, fast paced, and original. But Avi's treatment of *Romeo and Juliet* is also provocative. Why make Shakespeare's tragedy into a comedy? Is Avi taking a subtle moral stand as he illustrates positive outcomes for Romeo and Juliet instead of the gory suicides with which Shakespeare concludes? Is this novel his way of teaching against the ideology of the play? Or does *Romeo and Juliet Together (and Alive) at Last* forefront our hypocrisy? Despite all the carnage and sadness of Shakespeare's play, Romeo and Juliet are among the most universal and ubiquitous icons of romance in Western culture. Does the novel ask us to admit that we rarely pay attention to the story's "real" ending anyway? In Avi's refreshing inversion of tradition, students who study *Romeo and Juliet* don't learn much about tragedy, but readers of his novel may learn a great deal about themselves and their culture if they pause to ask, why not?

Romeo and Juliet as Adventure

In Geoffrey Trease's *Cue for Treason* (1940) the Romeo figure begins by fleeing into exile and doesn't find love until the conclusion of the novel. Reversing the elements of Shakespeare's story enables the author to focus on some of the smaller themes of the play—like friendship and rebellion—and to forefront adventure over romance. The novel begins in the late sixteenth century when the greedy Sir Philip Morton begins to enclose the common land traditionally reserved for the Cumberland farmers. Fourteen-year-old Peter Brownrigg joins in breaking down the new stone walls as an act of civil rebellion. Once his part in the crime is discovered, Peter must leave home until tempers cool. Stumbling upon a troop of traveling performers, Peter quickly makes a new life for himself as an actor. Competition from another recent addition to the company, thirteen-year-old Kit Kirkstone, keeps him on his toes until he discovers Kit is really a girl fleeing from an arranged marriage with the same villainous Sir Philip who wants to punish him. As with his Romeo, Trease reverses the events of the story for his Juliet. She runs from an unwanted marriage first and meets the boy of her dreams later.

During the first half of the novel Peter and Kit spend most of their time in the company of actors learning the ins and outs of the theatrical world and improving their skills as performers. At first the two compete. Eventually, Peter discovers Kit's identity and can only wonder at his own blindness. He spends half his time as a Shakespearean actor playing a girl disguised as a boy, but he never considers that life can imitate art. Peter says, "Afterwards, thinking back and remembering a dozen little things, I couldn't imagine why I'd never thought of it before, especially as the idea was always cropping up in the plays we acted" (67). Once Peter realizes Kit's extraordinary skill comes from real experience as a girl, the two begin cooperating. Surprised to realize that a girl can hike, ride, and skirmish as well as a boy, Peter even begins to sympathize with Kit's distress over the exclusion of women from stage performance. Kit insists, "Men are scared that women would act them off the boards if they were given the chance" (68). Peter challenges her point, but knows her performances draw more applause than his own.

Once the traveling season ends, Peter and Kit look for work among the famous companies of London. No one has work for two North Country boys until a young playwright offers Kit the chance to read the lines of his newest heroine, Juliet. Not surprisingly, Kit performs the role with great skill, and gossip spreads that the theater-goers of the city can anticipate a grand entertainment when the new play *Romeo and Juliet* premieres. The success of *Romeo and Juliet* leads to more work for the whole company. Together Peter and Kit play leading roles in *The Merry Wives of Windsor* as Anne Page and Mistress Quickly before Queen Elizabeth herself during the Christmas celebrations at court. Their theatrical careers come to a sharp halt, however, when Peter loses a play script. In an attempt to recover it from a thief, the two stumble upon a political conspiracy.

Throughout the second half of the book Peter and Kit hurry from London to Cumberland and back again, seeking information, rooting out traitors, and narrowly escaping death several times. Eventually, they unravel a plot to assassinate Queen Elizabeth during a command performance of *Henry V*. Using their skill as actors and their friendship with other members of the theatrical profession, Kit and Peter capture the villains and bring word of the plot to the court just in the nick of time. Afterwards, Queen Elizabeth herself gives the two young patriots an audience and rewards them for their services. Shakespeare's protagonists reach heroic stature by falling victim to the bloodthirsty conflicts of their elders; Trease's protagonists achieve the same status by protecting their elders from such conflicts. In this version of *Romeo and Juliet* the protagonists don't have to die to bring peace and accord to a disordered country. Instead, they get to marry and live happily ever after.

In addition to retelling *Romeo and Juliet* Trease's novel exhibits some of the features of historical fiction. Unlike those books discussed in Chapter 3, however, *Cue for Treason* includes some misleading material that limits its historical usefulness. Although the geographic detail of Cumberland (more often referred to as the Lake District today), the description of the political intrigues surrounding Elizabeth's court, and the representation of the theatrical profession all have much to recommend them, two other significant aspects of the novel are fraught with anachronism.

Trease misrepresents the prominence of the written word and attitudes toward literacy throughout the novel. The son of a local yeoman, a farmer who owns his land direct from the crown, Peter attends the local grammar school where he is being prepared, with several other scholars, for Queen's College at Oxford. This educational background might seem reasonable to modern readers but would have been extraordinary during the Renaissance. University education in this period prepared students to enter into professions in the church and government; there would be no reason (and no support) for a boy like Peter who loves the land to even consider such a tremendous shift in his circumstances. Later in the novel after Peter and Kit have joined the traveling actors, they are encouraged to write home to their people, "just to tell them [they're] all right" (57). Regular postal service and casual correspondence are not features of Renaissance England, especially for apprentices running from the law. Finally, Peter runs into trouble after he loans his copy of Shakespeare's newest play to a stranger who professes interest in reading the story. The stranger pleads, "I suppose you couldn't spare this copy, just for this evening? If I can't see it, I *should* like to read it" (99). Such scenes make theatrical scholars quiver! Actors with large roles may have received *sides*, a copy of their lines with cue words, and actors with small roles might have memorized their lines without ever seeing them in print. Under virtually no circumstances, however, would an apprentice have been entrusted with a complete copy of a script. The expense of reproducing scripts by hand and the need to protect plays from piracy meant most companies owned only two or three copies of any script. Trease litters his novel with casual forms of literacy. These anachronistic references make it hard for young readers to understand the differences between Shakespeare's world and our own. As Rebecca Barnhouse argues, it is often difficult for authors in a society that values literacy as highly as our own to represent a world in which reading and writing are merely incidental skills, valued less than practical knowledge and experience (Books and Reading 364–67).

Trease's heroine, Kit Kirkwood, also seems out of place in the novel. A wealthy heiress, Kit runs away from her guardians to avoid a marriage with Sir Philip who wants to join his lands with hers. Female heiresses were unusual in the Renaissance; the traditional practice of primogeniture made it very difficult for property, especially land, to belong to women. Even were Kit's status as an heir credible, her reaction to the marriage is not. Aristocratic weddings were frequently arranged to consolidate property and family ties; the opinions of the young bride and groom were not generally considered significant. In Trease's novel everyone from Peter to Shakespeare to Queen Elizabeth herself sympathizes with Kit's decision to avoid an unappealing match; such attitudes contradict historical practices. Making an appropriate marital alliance was a duty expected of those few people priveleged with wealth. Her eventual decision to marry a penniless yeoman's son strains credulity even further.

Finally, Kit's upbringing also seems too modern. Although she curtsies and plays the court lady with a practiced skill on stage that the other boy apprentices cannot match, she also shows herself to be an accomplished swimmer, climber, and equestrian. Most men didn't learn to swim during the Renaissance, let alone women. A young lady of aristocratic position might have enjoyed a few lessons with a tutor but would have spent most of her time learning the skills necessary to run an estate. As the lady of the house she might not need to collect eggs, bake bread, or card wool, but she would still need to supervise the management of the barnyard, the dairy, the kitchen, and the household. Kit's tomboy upbringing appeals to modern readers because it seems familiar, not because it is authentic. The recent Academy Award winning film, *Shakespeare in Love* (1998) actually provides a much more authentic vision of the plight awaiting a stage-struck young heiress. Like Kit, Viola yearns to act and hates her fiancé, yet she is forced both to give up theater and to wed according to custom.

Cue for Treason provides readers with the opportunity to explore a version of *Romeo and Juliet* with assertive, adventuresome, and optimistic protagonists. Unlike Shakespeare's characters, Peter and Kit refuse to be driven to extremes by fate; taking their own lives to avoid capture or separation never occurs to them. If their ability to outwit adult conspirators time and time again seems a bit unrealistic, Trease makes up for his excesses by constructing a very believable romance. This Romeo and Juliet do not fall eternally in love across a crowded room; their relationship grows out of competition, sympathy, and shared adventure.

Romeo and Juliet in Space—Star-Crossing Lovers

Anne McCaffrey's *The Ship Who Sang* (1969) takes the unusual opportunity of intermingling the classic genre of tragedy with the modern genre of science fiction; her vision of *Romeo and Juliet* demands more suspension of disbelief than the work of Belbin, Avi, or Trease but also invites more speculative thought and discussion. Famous for her series of novels about the dragon-riding colonists of the planet Pern, Mc-

Caffrey appeals both to her established fans and to most other readers of science fiction with this book. Her casual use of invented technical jargon may make the novel less interesting to readers without experience in the genre.

The Ship Who Sang can be interpreted as a sustained exploration of what it means to be Juliet. Born with extraordinary physical birth defects, McCaffrey's Juliet—named Helva—exists as an intellectual entity rather than a bodily one. She has been surgically implanted as the "brain" of a sophisticated space ship. Helva is partnered with a "brawn," a highly trained pilot who takes care of any tasks requiring physical mobility. Helva falls in love with Jennan, a brawn, not at first sight, but, fittingly, at first sound. With no sense of a physical existence, Helva values communication much more than appearance. Jennan likes to sing; his beautiful voice wins her. The barriers between Helva and Jennan are even more insurmountable than those between Romeo and Juliet. Jennan dies tragically—not because of his love for Helva, but in spite of it.

Helva's deep mourning nearly leads her to follow Juliet's example and commit suicide, but a chance encounter with two other desperate women, one a brawn and one a brain-ship like herself, enables her to recognize suicide as self-destructive, not as noble or sacrificial. Even though she has been having a difficult time recognizing the worth or meaning of her own life, she can easily see what the other women are giving up with their unwitting worship of death. Valuing the dead more than the living doesn't lead to freedom but to a kind of cult-like bondage that dishonors, rather than sustains, a lost love.

McCaffrey asks readers to consider the meaning of *Romeo and Juliet* most directly in the section of the novel entitled, "Dramatic Mission." Against her better judgment, Helva accepts the duty of transporting a small band of actors to perform for the Corviki, a newly discovered sentient race who are willing to trade secrets of the physical universe for the secrets of art. McCaffrey enjoys herself rehearsing age-old debates about the value of art. One cynical actress asks, "What possible significance could things like those Corviki find in Romeo and Juliet, an outmoded love story of an improbable social structure?" (94). But the director of the company has more faith in the play:

> The Bard has been translated into every conceivable language, alien and humanoid, and somehow the essence of his plays has been understood by the most exotic, the most barbaric, the most sophisticated. There is no reason to suppose that Will Shakespeare hasn't got something to say to the Corviki. (121)

As the actors begin to rehearse on the new planet among the Corviki, they begin to understand a new way of conceiving Shakespeare's play.

The dramas are powerful because they are, in essence, constructed of power. The Corviki experience all relationships as bursts of raw energy. The great emotions and conflicts of *Romeo and Juliet* become for them exchanges of energy—between sets of actors and between the audience and the performers. Narrating for the reader, Helva explains, "the atmosphere crackled, popped, boomed and thundered with the resultant explosions as immeasurable positive forces recombined and all the previously expended energy was reabsorbed" (127). Critics have often debated Ben Jonson's famous tribute to Shakespeare, "He was not of an age, but for all time." McCaffrey takes the discussion beyond the solar system and cleverly imagines a way that plays so deeply rooted in particular cultural practices might continue to have value for beings outside of, even alien to, Western culture.

Providing transport for the actors enables Helva to experience more intimate levels of *Romeo and Juliet* as well. When the actors discover that Helva is herself a lover of drama with the capacity to mimic a wide range of vocal tones, they enlist her as a performer. She reads various roles during rehearsals on the ship, and even joins them on the surface to play the role of the Nurse. All entities exist merely as energy on Corviki, enabling Helva to have a physical presence and set of experiences no different from that of the other humans. The opportunity tempts her. She could join the Corviki herself and become a form of pure energy as several of the actors do. Or, she could assume the abandoned body of one of the actresses; she could, literally, become Juliet. Helva, however, recognizes the limitations of the human form. Juliet is always doomed—Helva discovers she has no desire to play this role.

In the final episodes of the novel, Helva earns her independence and finds true love. With her new partner she heads out to explore the uncharted reaches of the universe. McCaffrey's novel manages simultaneously to take Shakespeare lightly and seriously. *The Ship Who Sang* uses newfangled gadgets, like brain ships, to update the timeless drama of a young woman coming of age. Interweaving elements of Shakespeare's tale into her story merely adds a kind of sophistication to her version. Yet, underneath the mechanical miracles and strange planets that serve as costumes and scenery for McCaffrey, she shows that developing an understanding of love without destroying a sense of self continues to be a challenging task.

Conclusions

Romeo and Juliet die, but their story doesn't. Examining the ways modern writers reimagine and reshape Shakespeare's tale has the potential to tell us a great deal about ourselves. Not one of the retellings discussed in this chapter ends with the death of both protagonists. Even *Westside Story* and *The Ship Who Sang* kill only the Romeo figure, and these two pieces seem designed for adult audiences at least as much as for young adult audiences. Shakespeare takes risks that even the most thoughtful modern writers seem hesitant to match.

On one level, we might interpret the happy (or at least still breathing) endings of these novels as evidence of social progress. We don't write books about suicide because we no longer wish to idealize or sentimentalize that kind of catastrophe. Or maybe it is denial—a version of self-censorship or bowdlerization intended to protect young adult readers from thinking about something as dangerous as suicide.

The asexual nature of the romances by Avi, Trease, and McCaffrey also merits consideration. Each of these authors sidesteps the electrifying lust so absolutely intrinsic to *Romeo and Juliet*. Why? How does avoiding consideration of physical attraction benefit young adult readers? The perversity of canonizing *Romeo and Juliet* and then refusing to acknowledge one of the very themes that makes it attractive to young audiences speaks volumes about our society. Only Belbin addresses the sexual magnetism between Romeo and Juliet directly.

Young adult readers may learn important lessons by studying the imagery of nights and knights in Juliet's Act 3, scene 2 soliloquy or by exploring the structures of male friendship among Romeo and his pals, but they might discover even more, especially about their world, by comparing Shakespeare's text with modern interpretations and exploring some of the questions posed here.

Chapter Five

Hamlet: Prince
of the Schoolyard

Hamlet seems like an especially ripe text for revision by young adult authors; the themes embedded in this single play serve as a virtual catechism for the field of adolescence: Hamlet dislikes his stepfather and fights with his mother; Ophelia's father thwarts her romance with Hamlet; two young men, Hamlet and Laertes, compete for prominence in the kingdom; Hamlet's childhood friends, Rosencrantz and Guildenstern, betray his trust; Hamlet contemplates suicide, and Ophelia appears to have indulged in it; Hamlet sees a ghost but cannot tell if it is credible; Hamlet even gets to have an escapade with pirates. Parental conflicts, romantic conflicts, peer conflicts, mystery, death, adventure— Shakespeare really packed this play full of crowd-pleasing favorites.

Consequently, many young adult novels without direct Shakespearean links make fine literary juxtapositions with *Hamlet*. In *From Hinton to Hamlet* (1996) authors Sarah Herz and Donald Gallo suggest several novels young adult readers may find particularly enlightening when read against the thematic backdrop of *Hamlet* (42–43). Bruce Brooks' *What Hearts* (1992) and Robert Cormier's *The Chocolate War* (1986) top their list. Brooks' novel follows the development of a precocious young boy named Asa who distrusts and dislikes his stepfather and finds the seventh-grade girl he loves completely oblivious to him. Life seems to be a series of dark disappointments for Asa. Cormier's famous novel is even grimmer. Cormier's protagonist, Jerry, and Shakespeare's Hamlet have few direct parallels, but as Herz and Gallo point out, both Denmark and Jerry's high school are tainted environments in which adult authority cannot be trusted (43). Jerry and Hamlet teeter on the verge of painful decisions; they must choose between self-protection through inaction or self-destruction when they confront evil. Both splendid novels in their own right, *What Hearts* and *The Chocolate War* bring many of the thematic concerns explored in *Hamlet* into modern environments.

Oddly, however, the thematic richness of *Hamlet* has inspired surprisingly few direct revisions of the play in young adult literature. Loose allusions to Hamlet and his difficulties appear with frequency— some of Hamlet's lines, like "To be or not to be" are so famous that authors can toss them casually into their prose with complete confidence that they will be recognized and appreciated. Sometimes these allusions offer minor commentary upon Shakespeare. Only three novels, among the many scoured in my research for this book, significantly develop a vision of *Hamlet* as part of their own stories.

Shadows of *Hamlet*

Katherine Paterson's Newbery Medal winning *Bridge to Terabithia* (1977) is a moving novel with thought-provoking tangential connections to *Hamlet*. Paterson's novel is particularly fascinating because it strikes an intriguing balance between conservative and subversive social attitudes. Most of *Bridge to Terabithia* seems like a cleverly subversive text because Paterson is clearly concerned with redefining the ways readers think about gender roles and socially constructed gender stereotypes. In the book two androgynously named and depicted characters struggle to develop and sustain an unexpected friendship. Jess, the novel's male protagonist, feels lost and betrayed by his family as he moves toward adolescence—he is a youthful version of Hamlet. His father is too physically exhausted by work and too emotionally distant to give his son the overt love and affection he desires. Jess' father isn't dead, as Hamlet's is, but he seems nearly as unapproachable. Like Shakespeare's Gertrude, Jess' mother shows genuine love for her son, but is far too consumed by other aspects of her life (in this case caring for four other children and running an economically deprived household) to pay much heed to her sensitive son. Even Jess' hobbies have betrayed him. Like Hamlet, Jess is drawn to artistic expression. Hamlet writes poetic love letters to Ophelia and enjoys spontaneously performing a dramatic speech when a troop of traveling actors visits the castle at Elsinore. Jess' preferred mode of artistic expression, drawing, is regarded as aberrant; the other boys his age like football and television. In order to win the appreciation of his family and schoolmates, Jess dedicates himself to becoming the fastest runner in the fifth grade. Hamlet too finds himself drawn into a masculine competition of physical strength in order to prove courage and worth. In both the play and the novel, the physical competitions go awry. Hamlet loses his contest because Laertes violates customary rules of honor and fences with a poisoned blade. Jess loses too. His dreams are abruptly destroyed when the new girl, Leslie, violates the playground rules and races with the boys—what is worse, she wins!

Leslie is as much of a misfit at Lark Creek Elementary as Jess, and she becomes his Ophelia. Her mother is virtually absent, like Ophelia's mother who is never even mentioned in *Hamlet*. Her father is too busy with his political writings (reminiscent of Polonius' profession as political adviser to the king) to pay her much heed. Eventually, the two become friends, introducing each other to new ideas and interpretations of the world—building their own kingdom. Like Hamlet and Ophelia, their families and friends suspect them of being girlfriend and boyfriend, but in this novel the love the two share for each other is much less stereotypical. One of Leslie's gifts to Jess is literature. She shares her books and tells him stories—including *Hamlet* (52)—surely an unusual choice for most fifth graders!

One day Jess is offered a trip to Washington D.C. Without explaining his absence to her, Jess abandons their plans and their kingdom. Hamlet, too, leaves Denmark suddenly and, apparently, without explanation to Ophelia. Hamlet leaves only at his uncle's insistence, whereas Jess views his day trip to the Smithsonian Museum as a glorious treat. Upon his return, each hero learns of his friend's death. Ophelia's body has been found floating in the brook. Gertrude delivers the news to the court:

> There on the pendant boughs her crownet weeds
> Clamb'ring to hang, an envious sliver broke,
> When down her weedy trophies and herself
> Fell in the weeping brook. . . .
> Till that her garments, heavy with their drink,
> Pull'd the poor wretch from her melodious lay
> To muddy death. (4.7.172–183)

Hamlet's grief nearly overwhelms him, and he jumps into the grave with the corpse. When Jess returns from his trip, he learns that Leslie's body has been discovered "down in the creek" (103). The rope swing she used to cross the ravine apparently broke and sent her to a wet and muddy death. Unlike Hamlet, however, Jess' unspeakable grief over his friend's accidental death eventually motivates his father to reach out to him, and the father and son are reconciled.

The ending of Paterson's novel exemplifies the tendency of writers revisioning Shakespearean plots to accept or at least acknowledge conservative social patterns. On one hand, Paterson forces readers to rethink their expectations about gender and condemns the social

pressures that mold and limit the behavior of children. Jess and his father, unlike Hamlet and the old King, survive the tale and are left with
the possibility of a newly sympathetic relationship. On the other hand,
Paterson, like Shakespeare, sacrifices Leslie, her Ophelia, in the service
of patriarchal paradigms—a thoroughly conservative choice. For Paterson, Shakespeare is a cultural icon—not necessarily because his stories
are the best—but because, despite ourselves, they are still true. Paterson's message or vision is only possible at the expense of the heroine.

Hamlet in the High School

Two more young adult authors who take *Hamlet* as their starting point,
Laura A. Sonnenmark and Lois Duncan, both set their novels in a high
school. Sonnenmark's revision of *Hamlet* suggests she might share the
opinion of many literary critics that Shakespeare's tragedies are awfully
grim material for young adult readers. Early in the novel Sonnenmark's
heroine sarcastically summarizes the jolly offerings of the Bard:

> First there was Othello, who is this crazy person who strangles his
> doormat of a wife in a fit of jealousy. Then there was Macbeth, who
> goes mad with ambition and kills all his houseguests. (Like the Roach
> Motel: You can check in, but you can't check out.) Of course, having
> a wife like Lady Macbeth would send anyone over the edge.
>
> And then there was my personal favorite, Hamlet, the melancholy
> prince of Denmark, who either kills or is responsible for the killing of
> virtually the whole cast. . . . And people complain about violence on
> television! The writers of *Nightmare on Elm Street* have nothing on
> Shakespeare, who certainly knew his blood and gore. (3)

Sonnenmark counters the serious tone of *Hamlet* by making it the centerpiece in a primarily comic story and by replacing the solemn protagonist of Shakespeare's play with a wry and witty female narrator.
Sonnenmark's *Something's Rotten in the State of Maryland* (1990) re-
lates Marie Valpacchio's development from crowd-pleasing compla-
cency to enthusiastic individualist. Marie neglects to fill out her class
registration card and finds herself assigned to Mr. Phillips' class in
Shakespeare's Tragic Heroes. She isn't impressed. Nor do the course
writing assignments appeal to her. Marie can choose between writing
a Shakespeare term paper, rewriting the last act of a play, writing a new
act for a play, or even writing an entirely new play. Marie chooses the
last—it involves neither research nor rereading—she can simply do
her own thing: "Why not a modern *Hamlet*? How hard could it be? The
story was already there; all I had to do was modernize it a bit and write
the dialogue" (5). Much to her surprise and chagrin, her play impresses

Mr. Phillips so much that he selects it for the winter production of the Magothy High School Thespian Society.

Marie's initial apathy toward the project grows gradually to enthusiasm and pride as she sees her drama take shape on stage and learns to enjoy the give and take of creative collaboration. As her friendships grow with the members of the drama club, especially Simon Conreith, the student director of the play, her old friendships become strained. Marie's boyfriend, Brian, resents how little time she has for him, and most everyone in the gang blames her when popular but vapid Ashley does not win the coveted role of Opal (the Ophelia character in Marie's updated *Hamlet*). As the pressure to choose between what is comfortable and what is challenging mounts, Marie is surprised to discover that the decisions aren't as difficult as she had feared.

The Shakespearean motifs in Sonnenmark's novel are never deeply developed. Marie's play, *Holden, The Prince of Culpeper County*, is a fairly superficial adaptation of *Hamlet*. To a large extent Marie has simply renamed each of Shakespeare's major characters with a typical modern name that shares the same initial as the original. Her substitution of "Holden" for "Hamlet" may be her most sophisticated shift, since it calls to mind Salinger's infamous hero from *The Catcher in the Rye*, who shares Hamlet's predilection for obsessive self-reflection and evaluation. Marie does little to change the plot of Shakespeare's play, other than allowing her Hamlet to survive. As Marie herself explains:

> Holden's father has recently died, and his mother remarried his uncle. Holden disapproves of his uncle, with good reason. Holden has a girlfriend, Opal, whose brother Luke is his best friend. Doing a bit of detective work, Holden finds out that his Uncle Claude killed his father so he could marry his mother and inherit the family fortune. But instead of going to the police or even just killing his stepfather, he goes a little crazy. He drives the people closest to him away—and treats Opal so horribly that she kills herself. In the end he finally does kill Uncle Claude, but it's too late. His whole life is ruined. (23)

Throughout the novel Marie, Simon, and the other members of the cast spend time debating the various motivations of the characters and how to convey these motivations on stage. They struggle with different solutions to the problem of Holden's knowledge—while Shakespeare begins his play with supernatural admonitions delivered by a ghost, they feel such a messenger would seem implausible in a modern adaptation. They also experiment with different reasons for Holden's (or Hamlet's) secrecy and what it might mean about his psychological state. Opal's (or Ophelia's) suicide also provokes a discussion. *Something's Rotten in the State of Maryland* does not provide many new insights into *Hamlet*, but it does represent students responding to the play in a convincing manner amidst the other dramas, big and small, of high school life.

Lois Duncan's *Killing Mr. Griffin* (1978) treats the issues raised in *Hamlet* much more seriously. Academic critics of *Hamlet* frequently discuss the play as a revenge tragedy, a genre which enjoyed a great deal of popularity at the end of the sixteenth century. Duncan focuses her novel on the question of revenge and the consequences of this activity upon both its victims and its perpetrators. Duncan's use of the play bears some faint but interesting resemblances to Paterson's. Both authors are concerned with the ways the rigid cliques and traditions of school life perpetuate some of the most limiting concepts of gender behavior. As discussed above, Paterson empowers her characters by using sexually ambiguous names and role reversals, but ultimately capitulates to tradition by sacrificing her Ophelia to the benefit of her Hamlet. Duncan's characters behave in much more traditional ways, but by conscientiously resisting the roles other people have written for them, her protagonists, especially her Ophelia and Gertrude, succeed in eluding their customary tragic fates.

Duncan's use of *Hamlet* is more sophisticated and a little harder to tease out of the novel than Sonnenmark's because she does not use a production of the play in her story or rely very much on one-to-one correspondences between Shakespeare's characters and her own. The novel opens in the English classroom of Mr. Griffin. Deeply committed to teaching his students discipline as well as literature and writing, Mr. Griffin is not very popular with his students. Several of them arrive without the day's assignment, a song written in Ophelia's voice. Blithe Betsy tries to plead ignorance, claiming she didn't understand the assignment. Athletic Jeff wants an extension; the previous evening's basketball game left him no time for homework. Responsible David watched the wind tear his homework out of his hands before school began. Mr. Griffin refuses to excuse any of them, and the anger that has been simmering all semester begins to coalesce into a plan.

Led by Mark, who flunked Griffin's course the previous term, Jeff and Betsy decide to kidnap their teacher; soon David is recruited to join them. Since Mark had originally suggested they actually kill Mr. Griffin, kidnapping sounds like a fairly harmless prank. After they have scared him and made him feel what it is like to be bullied and dominated, they'll let him go. With careful planning and masks, he'll never even be able to identify which of his students is to blame. The conspirators revel in their cleverness, envisioning an escapade they can brag about long after the glory years of high school have past. All they need is a decoy—someone to lure Mr. Griffin into staying after class until the parking lot has emptied and he can be attacked without witnesses. Mark suggests Susan.

Susan McConnell plays the lead role in Duncan's novel and serves as a parallel figure and commentary on Shakespeare's Ophelia. Her thoughtful response to Griffin's homework assignment indicates the close empathy she feels for Shakespeare's heroine:

> Where the daisies laugh and blow,
> Where the willow leaves hang down,
> Nonny, nonny, I will go
> There to weave my lord a crown.
>
> Willow, willow, by the brook,
> Trailing fingers green and long,
> I will read my lord a book,
> I will sing my love a song.
>
> Though he turn his face away,
> Nonny, nonny, still I sing,
> Ditties of a heart gone gray
> And a hand that bears no ring.
>
> . . .
>
> Water, water cold and deep,
> Hold me fast that I may sleep.
> Death with you is hardly more
> Than the little deaths before. (222)

Like Ophelia, Susan is besotted with the crown-prince of the kingdom, in this case David, who is the senior class president. Realizing her conscientious schoolwork and low social profile make her an unlikely suspect, Mark announces that they will invite Susan to serve as their decoy. Mr. Griffin will take her request for an after-school conference seriously. Susan's hopeless crush on David makes her easy to convince; all David has to do is ask her.

Aside from his prominent position in the school's social hierarchy, David shares several other characteristics with Hamlet. His sudden association with Susan is considered as incongruous and inappropriate as Hamlet's relationship with Ophelia. In Shakespeare's play, Polonius warns Ophelia to stay away from Hamlet and refuse his favors because he knows the heir to the kingdom can, and perhaps should, do "better" than his daughter. Betsy and the other seniors clearly feel the same way about mousy Susan; David is not in her league. They all suspect that he must be merely toying with her, as Laertes and Polonius suspect Hamlet, for the purpose of the greater plan. But Susan and David soon develop a genuine friendship, much as Hamlet and Ophelia's attachment is eventually revealed to be more than merely superficial.

Like Hamlet, David's father is absent. His mother and Gram, like Gertrude, are concerned with his welfare but, blinded by their own needs, make difficult demands on him. In the play, Hamlet tries to leave Claudius' court to return to school at Wittenberg. Only Gertrude's maternal pleas convince him to remain in Denmark. David's mother also wants him to spend as much time at home as possible. "Unless there's a reason," she tells him, "a real reason, it's nice for you to be at home in the afternoons. Your grandmother sits there alone all day, you know, and your homecoming at three is the high point of her day" (34). Both Hamlet and David seem to feel a bit trapped.

David's mother's attitude toward remarriage marks one interesting departure from Shakespeare's Gertrude. In the famous mousetrap scene in *Hamlet*, Gertrude remarks that the widowed queen who resists a new suitor "doth protest too much." Clearly her own swift remarriage stands as witness to how little protest she made to Claudius. David's mother, however, hasn't remarried. Raising her son and caring for a frail mother-in-law is a challenge, but, she says, "One marriage is enough for anybody" (35). This unusual opinion is one of the first clues Duncan gives her readers regarding the internal strength and self-sufficiency of her female characters.

Gram also seems at times like a minor version of Gertrude. Just as one of the most climactic scenes of *Hamlet* occurs in Gertrude's closet (an outmoded term for bedchamber), important revelations are made in Duncan's novel when David goes to confront his grandmother in her room. Like Gertrude, Gram becomes an accidental victim when the novel's plot spirals out of control.

Much of Hamlet's angst centers on his relationship with his lost father and his suspicions about his Uncle Claudius. Mr. Griffin simultaneously fulfills both of these roles for David in Duncan's novel. On one hand, David perceives Mr. Griffin as the villain who stands between him and his well-deserved destiny. David works hard in school; he recognizes education as his only real road to success. He knows he will need a scholarship in order to afford a college education. The poor grades handed out so liberally by Mr. Griffin threaten David's chance to win a scholarship to the University of New Mexico. David's sense of entitlement can hardly be considered selfish. He knows he will be the sole support of his mother and Gram once he reaches adulthood. His conscientious work in classes, on the debate team, and with student government seems about to be undermined by a single adult; his whole vision of the future has been unattractively rearranged by Mr. Griffin. David does not mind Mr. Griffin's high standards nearly as much as he resents his teacher's unwillingness to accept David's dutifully rewritten assignments. Hamlet feels the same way about Claudius in the play. Shakespeare never makes it clear whether Hamlet yearns for the throne, but audiences do get a strong sense of the protagonist's disillusionment. Hamlet's identity as a son, a prince, and a student are all threatened when Claudius unexpectedly asserts himself as King and father.

On the other hand, David begins to suspect that Mr. Griffin might be his long-absent father. David's vague memories of his father include a vision of the Stanford class ring he wore on his elegant hand, but he has neither seen nor heard from his father since the man abandoned the family to take up with a younger woman at least a decade earlier. After the students discover Mr. Griffin's dead body, David notices a very familiar ring on his teacher's hand. The police investigation, which follows Mr. Griffin's disappearance, also introduces David to Kathy Griffin, the English teacher's much younger wife. David never voices his suspicions about his parentage, but a number of his actions, like stealing the ring, disclose to the reader David's true feelings. By the end of the novel, David seems to have realized that the similarities between Mr. Griffin and his father are unlikely to be anything other than coincidental, but the sense of guilt he struggles with and the insecurity he feels about his revenge against a potential relative reminds readers of the doubt Hamlet feels as he regards both the ghost on the battlements and his Uncle Claudius. Neither hero knows whom to trust or in which direction truth lies.

Shakespeare makes much of the tensions that can run between fathers, brothers, uncles, sons, and nephews in *Hamlet*. The conflicts between old King Hamlet, Claudius, and Hamlet are echoed in the foil characters old Norway, Norway, and Fortinbras. Duncan hints at these kinds of family tensions too. As the novel unfolds, readers learn that Mark Kinney, the ring leader of the plot to kidnap Mr. Griffin, has lived with his uncle since his father died four years earlier. Later, Duncan reveals Mark's responsibility for that death. Mark operates as a kind of anti-Hamlet figure. He is embroiled in many of the same sorts of tensions and revenge plots as Hamlet, but whereas Shakespeare's protagonist acts carefully, thoughtfully, even hesitantly, Mark eagerly anticipates death and destruction. Hamlet, according to some critics, suffers from too large a conscience. Mark is a psychopath free from any moral inhibitions.

At the same time, Mark also reminds readers of Shakespeare's villains. Like Polonius, much of his information comes from covert observations. Jeff recalls how Mark's gaze pierced and followed him when they first met at age twelve; soon Jeff finds himself not so much Mark's friend as his follower. Mark recognizes how an upstanding student like David can be manipulated into joining the plot. Betsy and Jeff deride Mark's choice of a coconspirator, but Mark announces, "I know more about Dave than you do. He likes a challenge" (22). Mark is also the only one who notices Susan's crush on David, and more importantly, who recognizes how to use such a weakness. Like Polonius, who watches behind curtains and sets traps for Hamlet, Mark's observations and suggestions put the plot against Mr. Griffin into action. Unlike Polonius,

Mark seems poised to get away with his crimes and betrayals, but in the end he too is exposed and discovered.

Duncan's most revolutionary treatment of the *Hamlet* tale comes in her resolution of the novel. Susan, her Ophelia, recognizes, eventually, that she is little more than a disempowered pawn manipulated by Mark and, at least in part, by the others. In Shakespeare, Ophelia responds to the knowledge of betrayal and abandonment by first going mad and then dying. Gertrude's report of her death suggests Ophelia's drowning was accidental. The grave diggers make it clear they perceive her to be a suicide. Shakespeare leaves it up to directors, actors, and audiences to choose which interpretation to favor. Anguish and guilt torment Susan, but she embraces neither insanity nor death. Late in the book Susan recognizes that Mark's willingness to hide their role in Mr. Griffin's death extends to committing murder, and this knowledge finally convinces her that confession of their role in the original crime is the only acceptable course of action. She chooses to be a stronger and more assertive heroine than Ophelia. Her decision nearly comes too late, but nonetheless, this Ophelia survives the tragic disintegration of the kingdom.

In the last few pages of the book, Kathy Griffin suddenly comes to the fore. If Mr. Griffin works as both a revision of old Hamlet and of Claudius, Kathy Griffin is twice cast as Gertrude, the woman who married both Shakespearean characters. In the play, Gertrude frequently seems at best weak, passive, or dim and at worst sly, disloyal, and conniving. Very few interpretations of Gertrude find a heroic angle to her character. Duncan, however, turns this tradition on its head. Kathy Griffin trusts her husband. She suspects foul play as soon as Mr. Griffin goes missing. She sees holes and inconsistencies in the leads the police investigation turns up. She interviews witnesses herself and gradually begins to piece together clues the professionals have overlooked. This Gertrude discovers how her husband died—in time not only to save her own life, but to save the novel's Hamlet and Ophelia as well. Thanks to Kathy Griffin's interventions, the story is a tragedy, but not a blood bath.

Conclusion

The range of novelistic genres used to explore *Hamlet* stands as testimony to the many levels of Shakespeare's play—Paterson's gentle exposition of friendship and death, Sonnenmark's comic vision of high school, and Duncan's psychological thriller of revenge. Each presents a thoughtful method for exploring the play and offers a convincing vision of *Hamlet*'s themes. Together they serve as an argument for the richness of Shakespeare's play. The events in the castle at Elsinore may seem long ago and far away to many young adult readers, but when considered not as political or philosophical conflicts and instead as explorations of friendship, love, and revenge, the play seems distinctly more timely.

Chapter Six

Macbeth:
Who Cares About Kings—
Bring on the Witches!

There seem to be no characters who have attracted more attention from young adult authors than the three weird sisters of *Macbeth*. Who can say why? Perhaps the occult, by its very nature, even when used only as a stage device, cannot help but bewilder and entice us. Perhaps the witches' unresolved position in Shakespeare's play (we never hear what becomes of them) makes them better imaginative fodder for modern writers. Perhaps Shakespeare simply knew what he was doing; the concept of three women, frequently represented as a maiden, a mother, and a crone, who pull, spin, and cut the thread of life, teasing out man's fate, is at least as old as Greek mythology. This fascination with the witches is, in fact, by no means new. The earliest text we have of *Macbeth*, printed in the first collected edition of Shakespeare's works in 1623, shows signs of revision and collaboration. Many scholars suspect that several of the witch scenes, particularly the songs sung by the witches, were added to the play about five years after Shakespeare's company first performed it (Carroll 1999, 155–56). Renaissance playwrights often catered to their audiences; Shakespeare or a fellow author named Thomas Middleton probably added lines and songs only because the witch scenes were already popular with theater goers. Yet, our appetite for the witches apparently still remains unsatisfied.

Analyzing recent trends in writing, John Warren Stewig notes in a 1995 article, "One of the most interesting, recurring figures in recent fantasy for young readers is the witch woman" (119). Witch figures are, apparently, popular both on their own and as an aspect of canonical literature. Few young adult writers interested in reimagining *Macbeth* have been able to resist them. Instead of focusing on Macbeth and Lady Macbeth, most of these authors concentrate their literary revisions on the witches. The figure of the witch has long been, however, enticingly ambiguous; gender, morality, age, and power are all aspects of the witch open to interpretation.

Shakespeare's witches are themselves very elusive figures. In the dramatis personae of the play, they are referred to as weird sisters, but sometimes the characters call them witches. The ancient word *wyrd* (pronounced weird) refers to fate, the destiny that inescapably awaits every individual. The modern word *weird* still refers to the sense of strangeness fate and destiny can bring, but it has lost the aura of supernatural inevitability of its older ancestor. It is easy to see how magical creatures like witches could become associated with ideas about a man's wyrd, his fate, but witches are not quite the same things as weird sisters—the goddesses of fate. In using both the terms *weird* and *witch* to describe his characters, Shakespeare entangles audiences in a powerful but complex set of ideas. We cannot tell whether these creatures merely illuminate Macbeth's fate or whether their actions somehow change his fate—are they actors in the story or only observers of it? Is Macbeth a victim of the fates or a master of his fate?

Although for modern readers the word *witch* virtually always connotes an old, ugly woman, the term *witch* was not nearly so gendered in the Renaissance, when both men and women were all too frequently suspected of witchcraft. When Banquo first meets the three witches on the heath, he needs to ask:

> . . . What are these,
> So withered and so wild in their attire,
> That look not like th' inhabitants o' the earth (1.3.39–41).

He cannot even tell whether the creatures are women or not. In some ways they seem feminine, but they wear beards. Generations of Shakespearean directors have constructed a wide variety of solutions to this conundrum when producing the play. Mixed parties of male and female witches, heavily draped figures, trios of men, and trios of women have all been employed at various times. Interestingly, however, modern writers seem less flexible in their imaginations; trios of female witches uniformly people the pages of recent young adult novels revisioning *Macbeth*.

Representing witches in fiction for young readers can be a delicate task. Some conservative readers resist any discussion of witchcraft, believing such figures to be synonymous with demonic influences and devil worship. Some authors, perhaps in part as a response to such concerns, transform the witches from fearful figures into humorous and occasionally helpful caricatures. Treating the witches in this manner has a variety of effects. Sometimes it appears to diminish their role. Sometimes it merely distances readers from the figures highlighting their fictive qualities rather than focusing on potentially threatening aspects of the archetype.

Witches in Our World

Madeleine L'Engle, Penelope Lively, and Kate Gilmore provide interrogations of witches in their novels and all seem to share an interest in separating the damned arts of witchcraft from things imaginative or merely idiosyncratic. Neither L'Engle in *A Wrinkle in Time* (1962), Lively with *The Whispering Knights* (1971) and *The House in Norham Gardens* (1974) nor Gilmore in *Enter Three Witches* (1990) make the story of *Macbeth* the centerpiece of a plot, but all three authors seem to find inspiration for interesting female characters in Shakespeare's witches. L'Engle's book is much more deeply invested in *The Tempest,* as I discuss in Chapter 7, and Lively's novels borrow more from the traditions of ghost stories and folklore than the traditions of drama. Gilmore's novel weaves witch figures into contemporary urban life, but refrains from putting them into conflict with her male protagonist, as some interpretations of *Macbeth* seem to do.

In *A Wrinkle in Time* the three extraterrestrial companions to Meg Murry introduce themselves as three old women named Mrs. Whatsit, Mrs. Which, and Mrs. Who. Arriving on Earth near Halloween and forced for the sake of convenience to take up residence in a house reputed to be haunted, they decide to make the best of a bad situation and play the obvious roles. Materializing in front of Meg, Mrs. Which cannot resist embellishing her appearance with a broomstick and mimicking Shakespeare, "When shall we three meet again / In thunder, lightening, or in rain?" (60). But the three characters' resemblances to *Macbeth*'s weird women go much deeper. Mrs. Which, Mrs. Whatsit, and Mrs. Who appear to have control over time and space. The prophecies and gifts they outfit the three children with also seem to imply their knowledge of the future. And like the ambiguously powerful witches of Shakespeare's play, these three mystical creatures refuse to help the children directly. Most interesting, however, are the responses of the villains in *A Wrinkle in Time* to the three women.

Meg, Charles Wallace, and Calvin struggle to free Mr. Murry from imprisonment in Camazotz, a civilization characterized by conformity and oppression. In an attempt to undermine the children's confidence and divide their loyalties, the evil ruler of Camazotz tries to convince Meg and Calvin that their three extraterrestrial friends are little more than "witches" (142); it is the first time this frequently pejorative term is used in the book. Although Meg and Calvin are able to see the fallacies of the accusation fairly quickly, L'Engle subtly illustrates labeling and scapegoating as coercive tactics employed by those with evil intentions. In L'Engle's world idiosyncratic women, a description that applies equally as well to Meg and Mrs. Murry as it does to Mrs. Whatsit, Mrs. Which, and Mrs. Who, are not dangerous but necessary components of a free society. L'Engle draws her readers' attention to the ways that labels, like the term *witch*, can be unscrupuously used to denigrate or penalize a target, especially female targets. Her novel implies that heroes look beyond such labels and base their judgments on a person's actions and character, rather than being frightened off by rumors or slanders.

L'Engle's investigation of the use and abuse of the term *witch* is particularly significant in regard to *Macbeth*. Like all of Shakespeare's plays, *Macbeth* invites a variety of interpretations. Instead of reveling in this complexity, some audiences turn to misogyny. Attributing Macbeth's crimes to the women in the play, either Lady Macbeth or the weird sisters or both, even when Shakespeare's own language clearly avoids such oversimplifications, is common. Volumes of Shakespearean scholarship are devoted to questions about Lady Macbeth's maternal instincts (or lack of such instincts) and Macbeth's vulnerability to feminine wiles. More disturbing, however, is the evidence of this type of misogyny in children's editions. For example, in Mary and Charles Lambs' edition, Lady Macbeth is first introduced as "a bad, ambitious woman" (137). Readers are left with little doubt as to whom to blame in this version. In a 1997 article, critic John Stephens makes similar arguments in his assessments of other modern children's editions; he also points out that heightened descriptions of Lady Macbeth's seductive powers only tend to contribute to this kind of stereotyping (31).

Fortunately, not all authors fall into this trap. As early as 1900, E. Nesbit seems consciously to draw her reader's attention to the danger of scapegoating women. She adds historical material to her retelling of *Macbeth* to help justify Lady Macbeth's behavior:

> Lady Macbeth was the grand-daughter of a King of Scotland who had died in defending his crown against the King who preceded Duncan, and by whose order her only brother was slain. To her, Duncan was a reminder of bitter wrongs. Her husband had royal blood in his veins, and when she read his letter, she was determined that he should be king. (68)

Of course, these added historical tidbits are just as inaccurate a representation of Shakespeare's *Macbeth* as are versions that go out of their way to blame Lady Macbeth, but at least Nesbit demands that her readers draw independent conclusions about the ultimate villainy of each character rather than playing judge and jury by herself.

Penelope Lively includes allusions to Macbeth in two of her novels for young readers; she seems to have no trouble seeing the complexity with which Shakespeare draws his characters and enjoys exploring and exploiting it. Lively's *The Whispering Knights* (1971) would probably be most appropriate for readers teetering between children's novels and young adult fiction. Lively's novel borrows from the traditions of fantasy and time-slip adventure more than it uses the sharp realism and contemporary suburban and urban setting so typical in young adult fiction. But the relevance of *Macbeth* to a reader's full understanding and enjoyment of the book is clear as the novel opens with a trio of children, rather than the trio of witches who open the first scene of Shakespeare's play. These children are engaged, nonetheless, in a very familiar conjuring project:

> The frogs' legs were less appalling than the children had expected. They slid out of the tin with a plop, a slimy, grey-brown mass: very nasty, not obviously legs. Martha was much relieved. She had expected pathetic little webbed feet at the ends.
>
> "Seven and six for that lot!" said William with disgust. "I jolly well hope they're worth it."
>
> Susie began stirring the saucepan. The frogs' legs quickly disintegrated and merely served as a kind of thickening. The pictures were coming to pieces too. The bird's wing floated suddenly to the surface and Martha averted her eyes.
>
> "Are you sure it's all right?" she said uneasily. "I wish we'd never done it."
>
> "Course it's all right, silly," said Susie, her eyes on the pan. She stirred more vigorously and began to chant:
>
> "Double, double toil and trouble,
> Fire burn, and cauldron bubble."
>
> . . . Martha sat back on her heels, twisting a strand of hair nervously round and round her finger. She'd had doubts about this business, right from the start, but the others had insisted and, as usual, her fears had got brushed aside. It was a scientific experiment, William had said, not a spell. (8)

The first chapter goes on to explain the inventive and amusing ways the three children have procured all the things needed for the spell.

> Eye of newt and toe of frog,
> Wool of bat, and tongue of dog,
> Adder's fork, and blind-worm's sting,
> Lizard's leg and howlet's wing. (Shakespeare, *Macbeth* 4.1.14–17)

All of these less than ordinary ingredients present quite a challenge, and William, Martha, and Susie are driven at times to make some strange substitutions. In the end, however, the spell seems to work. They conjure a magical threatening force. And the rest of the novel chronicles their battle against the strange, dark force—one which has had many names at different times but always seems to remain feminine— Morgan le Fay, Duessa, Circe, the Witch in Snow White, and the evil in *Macbeth.* But this nameless or many-named force, much like the prophecies and apparitions in Shakespeare's *Macbeth,* can usually be seen by only the children, by those who have called it or sought it. In *The Whispering Knights,* as in *Macbeth,* questions about coincidence, fate, and the importance of individual will and determination are explored.

Some of the other themes and issues of *Macbeth* are explored in the lives of the children. Unlike Macbeth, these three friends remain true to each other, recognize the dark forces they have inadvertently invoked are imaginary or too powerful for them to control, and eventually manage to return to their "normal" lives and pursuits. Aside from the opening chapter, Lively's story does not make many overt references to Shakespeare's *Macbeth,* but for readers familiar with the play and its themes, the novel provides a terrific opportunity for exploring the consequences of curiosity and temptation in a modern setting, and perhaps, more importantly, of exploring these issues with young protagonists.

Lively also alludes to *Macbeth* in *The House in Norham Gardens* (1974). In this book orphaned Clare Mayfield lives with her two elderly and eccentric aunts in a North Oxford suburb. The center of the plot revolves around Clare's discovery of a *tamburin,* a ceremonial shield or ancestor mask from New Guinea, but a much smaller train of secondary plot events ties Clare to Shakespeare. She is cast as a supernumerary in a school production of *Macbeth.* Bored by her nameless, faceless appearances on stage, Clare decides to give herself a character. She decides to play her part as if she were Lady Macbeth's mother. And as she grows more invested in this self-created role, she becomes more convinced that Lady Macbeth's mother would never have sat silently through the banquet scene. On opening night, her ad libbed lines may add a new realism to the scene, but her more conventional classmates fail to appreciate them. Lively's use of Shakespeare in this novel is noteworthy not because of its complexity or quantity, but because of its suggestive ingenuity. In giving even this small voice to Lady Macbeth's mother, Lively implicitly joins the ranks of critics who argue that there is more going on with the women of the play than meets the eye.

Kate Gilmore's *Enter Three Witches* (1990) provides the most radical and friendly rereading of Shakespeare's infamous trio. Bren West lives in a Brownstone near Central Park, New York, with a trio of witches. His mother, Miranda West, and grandmother, Rose, both practice their arts commercially providing apparently legal (and ineffectual) spells and seances to interested consumers (their principles prevent them from accepting payment for their real magic). One of the household's borders, Louise LaReine, practices black obeah involving chickens and details best left unreported to the authorities. Together they form a trio of witches. Bren does his best to maintain a pretense of normality; he doesn't share the feminine power of witchcraft. He plays Frisbee with his dog Shadow, plots to reunite his parents (temporarily separated), and struggles to convince his mother to stop interfering with his life— he doesn't want to be summoned telepathically or to be sent frog gathering.

Despite his unusual family, Bren's problems are caused by a rather mundane affliction. He falls in love. Since Erika, Bren's beloved, has been cast as a witch in the school production of *Macbeth,* Bren decides to help his friend Eli design the lighting for the production. The romance progresses rapidly until Erika insists on visiting Bren's home. Bren has no intention of introducing Erika to his unorthodox family. His mother and grandmother also display a growing interest in the upcoming production of *Macbeth* and offer their services as consultants. They are very enthusiastic about Shakespeare's witches, but skeptical of a high school's ability to interpret and present them with an appropriate grandeur (14). Bren's attempts to keep his family and his romance secret from each other lead to a series of mishaps that not only alienate Erika, but nearly result in his banishment from the lighting board of *Macbeth.* Fortunately, Erika's curiosity leads her to discover Bren's secrets on her own, and to his delight she is uncritical of his peculiar family background. His mother's decision to add spice and authenticity to the special effects in *Macbeth* behind his back annoys Bren, but as her appearance at the performance also has the effect of rekindling the romance between Miranda and her estranged husband, Bren forgives her. Furthermore, the romance will distract her, and Bren is assured, at least temporarily, of some privacy and independence.

Miranda West's witchcraft can be interpreted as an exaggerated version of maternal instinct. Her magical interference operates on one level as a metaphor for the mundane meddling most teenagers suffer at the hands of their parents. More generally, however, Gilmore presents witchcraft as a potent modern possibility, and she refrains from labeling witchcraft with moral terms. Miranda's and Rose's magic seems mostly amusing, a version of the arts practiced by Samantha in the television classic *Bewitched.* LaReine's craft seems more sinister, maybe because she seems to take her work more seriously, but she never actually does any damage. Gilmore judges individuals by their actions rather than their allegiances. Whereas some interpretations of *Macbeth* pit the Scottish King against the dangerously mysterious feminine forces

of fate, in *Enter Three Witches* Bren learns to see the magical powers of
women as appealing and complementary forces, which along with his
own will and talents help shape his physical and emotional world.

A World of Witches

Terry Pratchett's fantasy novel, *Wyrd Sisters* (1989), takes readers to
the kingdom of Lancre in a place called the Discworld, where witches
need no particular explanation. Although Pratchett's work is not generally marketed as young adult literature, the energetically humorous
worlds of his creation are very popular with younger readers as well as
adult ones; in fact the positive response of his readers inspired Pratchett to write several other Discworld novels, including *Lords and Ladies,*
which revises *A Midsummer Night's Dream,* and is discussed in Chapter 9.
Pratchett's use of *Macbeth* is by far the most complex and sustained of
the novels yet examined in this chapter. The book begins with a scene
that clearly echoes the initial gathering of the three witches in Shakespeare's play, but in Pratchett's hands, the scene has had, or has suf-
fered, a facelift and head-to-toe renovation:

> The wind howled. Lightning stabbed at the earth erratically, like an
> inefficient assassin. Thunder rolled back and forth across the dark,
> rain-lashed hills.
>   The night was as black as the inside of a cat. It was the kind of
> night, you could believe, on which gods moved men as though they
> were pawns on the chessboard of fate. In the middle of this elemental
> storm a fire gleamed among the dripping furze bushes like the mad-
> ness in a weasel's eye. It illuminated three hunched figures. As the
> cauldron bubbled an eldritch voice shrieked: "When shall we three
> meet again?"
>   There was a pause.
>   Finally another voice said, in far more ordinary tones: "Well, I can
> do next Tuesday." (5)

In this novel, Granny Weatherwax, Nanny Ogg, and Magrat are drawn
into the politics of the small kingdom of Lancre. Each of these three
characters (the crone, the mother, and the maiden, respectively) is an
overdrawn caricature of one sort of witch. Granny Weatherwax is hard
and bony, dresses in black, and generally believes in sticking to tradition when it comes to her profession. Nanny Ogg is a lusty, rollicking
widow. Her magic is more frequently guided by self-interest and nepo-
tism than anything else. Magrat is the youngest of the three, and she is
very anxious to organize a coven—she yearns for moonlit dancing,
mystical ceremonies honoring the powers of creation, and a healthy in-

tegration of physical and spiritual powers. Her vision of witchcraft looks a lot like Glinda the Good distributing granola bars.

After the reigning king is murdered, the three witches find themselves in possession of the infant heir to the throne—whom they promptly palm off on a troop of traveling actors. Before he grows old enough to return and claim his throne, the new tyrant and his wife reveal themselves to be a melodramatic and even more dangerous version of Macbeth and his spouse (although this tyrant's name, like that of most of the characters in the play, differs from those used by Shakespeare). Pratchett enjoys himself collapsing the characteristics of Macbeth and Lady Macbeth into his tyrant. Here the King suffers from obsessive hand-wringing and other psychosomatic ailments. The witches are forced to take action to remove the despot and bring the real heir to the throne, or at least someone with enough political skill to mind his own business and leave the subjects of Lancre in peace. Elements of *Hamlet* and various folktales and stories are also woven into the fabric of the novel to create a complex tapestry of intertextualities, but throughout the book, the guiding narrative is Shakespeare's *Macbeth*.

Pratchett's novel shifts the premises and problems raised in *Macbeth* just enough to throw everything a little bit off kilter. In this novel the witches are powerful, but not complete mistresses of fate. Instead of watching Macbeth struggle against destiny, Pratchett asks readers to join in the witches fight to sustain control of the kingdom. Instead of creating three indistinguishable witches, he gives readers three distinctly individual ones whose specific characteristics complicate the plot. Instead of focusing on the tragedies resulting from selfish and tyrannical rule, Pratchett looks at the comic machinations arising from behind-the-scenes government intervention. Although some critics and teachers are tempted to dismiss Pratchett along with most authors of pulpy science fiction and fantasy novels, enjoying his tale actually depends upon very sophisticated reading and interpretive skills. Pratchett may seem irreverent toward the classics, like Shakespeare, but his novels reveal a detailed knowledge of literature, and he invites his readers to share at least a portion of this literary cultural background. He sees himself as part of a long tradition of story—though perhaps it would be fair to label him as one of the more amusingly idiosyncratic members of the literary family.

Discussing Pratchett's work in relation to young adult readers, literary critic John Stephens argues:

> Pratchett's handling of story also exemplifies a major importance of his work for the reading experience of adolescent readers: for a reader who has developed some sophistication in literacy, the text has the potential to stretch and expand reading ability and critical literacy. At the

level of story, for example, it encourages readers to pay close attention
in reading for the sense, and to develop skill in making connections
across extensive stretches of narrative. (1997, 33)

Ultimately, what makes Pratchett's accomplishment so noteworthy is
his ability to demonstrate these aspects of critical reading while providing an entertaining romp through a literary classic. Pratchett's novels illustrate that examples are almost always more fun than vocabulary lists
and lectures. What's more, Pratchett returns Shakespeare to his roots.
Today, Shakespeare connotes elite knowledge and cultural sophistication, but in his own era, Shakespeare built his reputation by appealing
to the common crowds; so too, in many ways, does Pratchett.

Bad Witches

Welwyn Wilton Katz is the only young adult author to concentrate her
novelistic energies on recuperating Macbeth's personal reputation. She
is also the only author who envisions Shakespeare's weird sisters as
mistresses of an evil force. In *Come Like Shadows* (1993), Katz imagines
an alternate history—one in which Macbeth rules Scotland well and
honestly after overthrowing a blood-thirsty Duncan and before being
destroyed by a treacherous Malcom. The novel opens on the eve of his
destruction in 1057 as Katz's Macbeth gives in to temptation and visits
the three witches who worship the Goddess. He is himself a follower of
Christ and has in the past refused the favors offered by the witches. Instead of making an unholy bargain with them to save his kingdom,
Macbeth inadvertently interrupts them in the middle of a ceremony involving an ill-informed young woman and a looking glass. Macbeth
and the oldest of the three witches end up trapped in the looking glass
and thrust far into the future. Over the centuries, the glass changes
hands, but it eventually ends up among the props used by Shakespeare's
company.

Although Macbeth lacks the magical knowledge to escape the mirror, the old witch can exit and enter at will. One of her first acts when
she discovers herself transported to London in 1606 is to interfere with
Shakespeare's manuscript of *Macbeth*. She cannot bear to see the man
who ruined her spell so long ago celebrated as a hero, so she ensures
that the drama portrays him as a villain, and thus she succeeds in twist-
ing and warping Macbeth's reputation all the way into the present day.

After establishing this quasihistorical background and conflicted
relationship between Macbeth and the witches, Katz's novel shifts to
contemporary Stratford, Canada, where sixteen-year-old Kinny O'Neil
has procured herself a very highly sought-after summer internship

helping the acclaimed director Jeneva Mackenzie with a production of *Macbeth*. Kinny soon learns that this production will attempt to highlight the political relevance of *Macbeth* by using costumes and sets, which suggest one of Canada's own civil battles in 1759 between the historical figures of Wolfe and Montcalm. Reverberations from this conflict still shake Canadian politics in the shape of language debates and the question of how both English- and French-speaking citizens can share governance of Quebec. Kinny can barely suppress her disappointment with Jeneva's politics and directorial decisions as rehearsals progress. Her opinions are shared by a young actor named Lucas who plays the role of Fleance.

Kinny does find Jeneva's philosophical interpretation of the play compelling. As Jeneva explains to the company early in rehearsals:

> "The Scottish play isn't just about a man who kills a king and takes his place," Jeneva went on. "It isn't even solely about his motivation: his ambition, his fascination with witchcraft, his dark love for the wife who persuades him to murder King Duncan. I think this is a play about power. Power. Who has it, who wants it, who takes it, who abuses it. And who is defeated by it." (68)

Lucas feels the power of the play as a special and inescapable pull toward the character of Macbeth. Macbeth's psychology entrances him. Unlike many murderers, Macbeth is smart and has a conscience; he retains his humanity even when he behaves despicably (41). Lucas finds himself driven to search out historical accounts of Macbeth; he wants to discover the man behind the play. The more Lucas learns, the more his admiration and belief in Macbeth's goodness grows.

Kinny spends her time searching for props—specifically a small mirror needed on stage near the closing scene of the play. Eventually she finds a strange, antique looking glass in a small shop called Things Past. Although they cannot explain it, both Kinny and Lucas find themselves drawn to stare into the depths of the mirror. Both see dark and ominous scenes and faces staring back. The powers of the play grow intertwined with the powers in the mirror.

A series of accidents distracts Kinny and Lucas. Early in rehearsals, an electrical accident kills the woman playing the lead witch and a few weeks later the star playing Macbeth is killed during a combat rehearsal. The well-known curse surrounding *Macbeth* seems to hold the Canadian production tightly in its grip. Opening night brings no relief. The politically inspired interpretation of the play garners only angry responses from both audiences and critics. The company looks with relief toward taking the production on tour in Scotland. Kinny, however, fears that she understands the cause of these crises—something evil in the mirror both offers her and threatens her with unspeakable powers,

and so she is unsurprised when a fire destroys even their Scottish theater. Slowly but surely, Kinny feels herself drawn to the heath where
hundreds of years earlier Macbeth himself confronted the witches. Lucas' growing empathy for Macbeth draws him to the heath as well.

As the novel reaches its climax in a scene echoing Macbeth's own
confrontation with the witches so many hundreds of years earlier, the
theme of power returns to the fore. Each character is forced to make
moral decisions regarding power and demonstrate how much he or she
desires it and what he or she is willing to sacrifice in order to attain it.
Kinny escapes the clutches of evil, Lucas finds his faith in Macbeth's essential nobility rewarded, and Jeneva MacKenzie disappears into the
mirror to become one with the trio of power-hungry witches.

Although Katz, unlike the other authors, sustains Shakespeare's focus on Macbeth as the central character in her novel, she removes any
ambiguity from Shakespeare's story. Audiences of the play generally
struggle to decide whether Macbeth is a victim of fate or whether he
deserves his fate. Katz resolves this conundrum solely in Macbeth's
favor. Not only is he exonerated of his crimes, but a horror of female
ambition and power is emphasized well beyond anything in Shakespeare's play. Instead of making Lady Macbeth a scapegoat as some of
the children's editions of Shakespeare discussed earlier, Katz eliminates Lady Macbeth and concentrates her scrutiny upon the witches.
Katz is unusual in her decision to create female deities that compete effectively with Christianity; even at this novel's end the worshippers of
the Goddess survive and seem likely to pursue their own powerful beliefs indefinitely. They do not threaten Christianity, but they are not
destroyed by it either—instead they seem to exist alongside it. But as
intriguing as is this willingness to consider a pagan form of worship on
the same plane as Christianity instead of merely as an extinct predecessor, her insistence on representing successful, ambitious women,
like Jeneva Mackenzie, as vengeful and evil undermines the innovation
of her vision.

The Real Dangers of *Macbeth*

Sharon Draper's *Tears of a Tiger* (1996) may not be as stylistically satisfying as Lively's novel, or as wickedly witty as Pratchett's zany tale, but
it may be the most provocative and most courageous novel in its use of
Shakespearean allusions. In *Tears of a Tiger* Draper draws attention to
the potentially negative qualities of a much revered and long-standing
literary classic, daring to imply that Shakespeare may no longer be worthy of his reputation. In so doing, Draper confronts head on one of the
criticisms most frequently and most vehemently levied against young

adult literature—the contention that it is too depressing, too shocking, and too pessimistic to be worthy of inclusion in a school curriculum. *Tears of a Tiger* is riddled with exactly these qualities, but Draper illustrates that desperation, disturbances, and distrust are not solely the provenance of young adult literature; they are instead among the staple qualities of much of the classical canon as well. In her novel, the protagonist reads Shakespeare's *Macbeth*—but instead of finding it remote and meaningless, the protagonist sees it as an echo of his own life and experience, and, even worse, he takes *Macbeth* as his role model.

Draper's novel opens with a newspaper article detailing a drunk driving accident that results in the death of one of the teenage boys riding as a passenger in the car. The novel follows and explores the consequences of this death, especially in the life of seventeen-year-old Andrew Jackson, who was driving the car and could only stand helplessly by in the moments following the crash as his best friend burned to death.

The novel is very grim—not only is Andrew riddled with guilt and despair, but most of the people in his world are too driven by their own fears or too overwhelmed by their own problems to understand his pain. Andrew's high school is not a simple or happy world; it is a very complex place.

The novel's narrative structure is in some ways reminiscent of that of a drama. As in a play, there is no single narrative voice controlling the audience's perspective. Instead, the novel is told through a collage of voices—snippets from Andrew's conversations with his basketball coach, entries from the diary of a classmate, assignments turned in for English class, letters, excerpts from counseling sessions.

In the middle of the novel one brief chapter recounts a morning's class discussion in Andrew's English class:

> —All right, class. We've almost finished our study of *Macbeth*. We've watched Macbeth change from a noble, trusted, dedicated soldier, willing to sacrifice his life for king and country, to a wretched, depraved, corrupt murderer who no longer has feelings of guilt or morality . . .
> —Mrs. Blackwell, does he die at the end?
> —Well, Marcus, he's just about dead inside already. He's got one little spark left—his refusal to surrender to Macduff and the forces of good—but don't you think his death is inevitable, Marcus?
> —Yeah, he deserves to die—he killed his best friend, he killed women and children, he killed the king. Yeah, I'd say my man deserves to die.
> —Okay, what about his wife? Does she deserve to die too? Mary Alice?
> —Well, it *was* originally her idea. If it hadn't been for her, Macbeth never would have killed the king in the first place. Women have that power over men, you know. Right, Keisha?

—Right on, girl. Now you're talking!

—Ooh—You wish! You livin in la-la-land ladies!

—Okay, Gerald, that will be enough. Keisha and Mary Alice have a right to their opinions too, you know. But Lady Macbeth who seemed so strong at the beginning of the play, had a rather rapid mental deterioration—remember she was walking and talking in her sleep and washing her hands uncontrollably? She finally cannot stand the pressure of the guilt, and she kills herself.

—Kills herself? What a wimp! I'm disappointed. I thought she was pretty cool for a while there.

—Sorry, Keisha. She takes the coward's way out by committing suicide and leaves Macbeth to face the end alone. But you must remember that she *was* a murderer. I don't think Shakespeare meant for her to be a hero. (106–07)

As the classroom discussion of death and responsibility grows more focused, Andrew grows more despondent. It becomes clearer and clearer how deeply he is beginning to sympathize with the protagonist of Shakespeare's play. Andrew feels that he has also unwittingly made the shift from a loyal friend and a respected member of the community to a corrupt murderer—isolated and ashamed. Like Macbeth, self-knowledge has come too late. His is a tale told by an idiot, full of sound and fury, signifying nothing. Not every reader interprets the ending of Shakespeare's play the same way. For some audiences, Macbeth retains at least of shred of nobility throughout the play—because he never gives up; in the face of overwhelming odds and terrifying prophecies, he fights on. Other audiences interpret the ending of Macbeth less optimistically—they see only despair in Macbeth's final actions. He isn't fighting death; he is embracing it.

The end of *Tears of a Tiger* makes it clear that Andrew is one of these pessimistic readers. Unable to see any hope or escape for Macbeth, and hence for himself, Andrew commits suicide. His tragedy is at least as poignant as that of the famous Scottish King. Draper's novel reminds teachers of the need to be careful what we wish for—students who take Shakespeare seriously may be in danger. She also subtly suggests that curriculum critics wary of presenting a painful or depressing world vision to students should examine traditional classroom materials with as much scrutiny as popular modern literature typically receives.

Conclusions

As Draper's novel reminds us, Macbeth has more to offer readers than witches, but a simple survey of the seven texts discussed in this chapter clearly reveals which characters most frequently grab the attention of modern writers. In many ways this concentration on witches and varieties of female power provides a needed counterpoint to the typical study of Shakespeare, which cannot help centering on forms of masculine power. Both the patriarchal social patterns of Renaissance England and the traditional prohibition against female stage performers contribute to the fact that women simply do not receive nearly as frequent or as complete a consideration in Shakespeare's plays (or those of any other Renaissance dramatist) as do men.

The small range of characters explored in these novels is balanced a bit by the range of genres authors reinterpreting *Macbeth* have embraced. Contemporary realism, science fiction, fantasy, and suspense are all represented among the works discussed here. If at first these genres seem less demanding or important than tragedy, the genre Shakespeare selected for his version of *Macbeth*, John Stephens' eloquent arguments for the curricular value of Pratchett's *Wyrd Sisters* should put such concerns to rest. In his theoretically elaborate and convincing article, Stephens suggests a list of the literary capabilities enhanced by thoughtful revisions, which seems designed to warm the heart of anyone struggling to find a place for contemporary literature in classrooms dominated by the demands of proficiency tests and mandated exams:

> reading for sense; reading for significance and theme; understanding how theme unifies and integrates narrative; grasping the textual and cultural effects of working across the boundary between 'high' and 'popular' culture; understanding how language and narrative construct or distort reality; grasping the point of the constructedness of fictional characters; developing awareness of the key principles of verbal humour; understanding genres; understanding the important textual functions of intertextuality and metafiction; and possessing a wide and expanding vocabulary. (37)

And in addition to all of these skill-enhancing attributes, revisions of Shakespeare's witches, like those of his other characters, have the immeasurably valuable quality of providing enjoyment to readers.

Chapter Seven

The Tempest:
Coming of Age
in a Brave New World

Master: Boatswain!
Boatswain: Here master; what cheer?

William Shakespeare (c. 1611)

There was a certain island in the sea, the only inhabitants of which were an old man, whose name was Prospero, and his daughter Miranda, a very beautiful young lady.

Mary and Charles Lamb (1807)

Prospero, the Duke of Milan, was a learned and studious man, who lived among his books, leaving the management of his dukedom to his brother Antonio, in whom indeed he had complete trust.

E. Nesbit (1900)

The Tempest *is a story of magic and monsters, and of an enchanted island set in a distant sea.*

Marchette Chute (1956)

Far, far away, upon the shore of a strange island that was forever wrapped in mists that the sun changed into moving curtains of gold, there sat an aging man and his young, lovely daughter.

Leon Garfield (1985)

It was like the frenzy of a raging animal, this dark fury of wind and sea that seized the ship.

Beverley Birch (1993)

The tempest raged, the storm roared, the sky was split by lightning and beneath it a tall ship was tossed about on a bubbling sea.

John Escott (1996)

Once upon a time there was an enchanted island, a green and lovely place, set in the great sea that lies between Europe and Africa.

Ann Beneduce (1996)

Despite the fact that *Romeo and Juliet* and *Hamlet* are most often considered as appropriate Shakespearean fare for young adult readers, *The Tempest* almost certainly has more to offer. The opening lines from Shakespeare's original and seven adaptations of the play for young readers quoted above speak convincingly of the range of emphases and interpretations this drama invites. Some authors are seduced by the fairy-tale qualities of the story—a king and a princess shipwrecked on an island. Some authors are charmed by the moral fable embedded in the plot—an old man learns the rewards of offering and accepting forgiveness. Still others are enticed by the elements of adventure—raging seas and usurpations and malformed monsters.

The Tempest, as Stephen Orgel argues in his 1987 critical introduction to the play, "is a text that looks different in different contexts" (11). In recent years critics, readers, and actors have wrestled with the questions of whether Prospero is benign or tyrannical, whether Caliban is servile or abused, and whether Miranda is dutiful or rebellious and with questions about why different audiences and interpreters have reached different conclusions about these issues. Perhaps no other play better demonstrates the ambiguities and opportunities for interpretive choices than *The Tempest*. One way to understand the interpretive effects of the sorts of changes made by the editors of Shakespeare for young people is to take a close, but quick, look at a single well-known edition of the play—Mary and Charles Lambs' tale.

Mary and Charles Lambs' version of *The Tempest* in *Tales from Shakespeare* (1807) is important both because of its status as one of the very first Shakespearean texts for a young audience, (as in the 1623 Folio it stands first in the Lambs' collection—increasing its likelihood to be read), and because of its staying power. The Lambs' collection has remained readily available ever since its initial publication nearly two hundred years ago.

The Lambs' edition makes two major interpretive choices. Their version begins by removing or absolving Prospero of any guilt or moral ambiguity. Whereas Shakespeare carefully creates a complex and challenging protagonist, the Lambs seem just as carefully to present a morally upright one. Prospero's practice of magic, an art frequently associated with the devil (especially during the Renaissance), is carefully and inaccurately justified as "a study at that time much affected by all learned men"(1). The harsh treatment of Caliban is renegotiated as merely "vexatious tricks" and is attributed entirely to Ariel who "took rather too much pleasure in tormenting" (2). Finally, the Lambs take full advantage of the interpretive necessities of narrative form mentioned in Chapter 1. They attribute motives and feelings to their characters that would normally be left to the actor or reader to interpret. They write, "'Pardon me, dear Master,' said Ariel, ashamed to seem ungrateful; 'I will obey your commands.'" And suddenly, due to the Lambs' addition of words like "ashamed" and "ungrateful," Ariel's complaints about a life of servitude are demonstrated to be limitations of his own character rather than evidence of Prospero's tyrannical, or at least demanding, rule. The Lambs' choices subdue the ambivalences so common in Shakespeare's play to create a benevolent and paternal interpretation of Prospero.

The Lambs' second important interpretive decision is to reduce substantially the themes of vengeance and betrayal in the play. They describe Caliban as "a strange misshapen thing, far less human in form than an ape" (2). Shakespeare, conversely, gives actors very little information about Caliban's appearance. The terms used to describe him, like "monster," are terribly vague. They might easily refer to his odor (unpleasantly fish-like) or his face or his clothing. The Lambs also eliminate Caliban's claims to the ownership of the isle and his reported attempt to rape Miranda. Rather than a threat or a competitor to Prospero's status as ruler of the island or to Ferdinand's position as Miranda's preferred suitor, Caliban becomes merely an oddity. When called to prepare food for the assembled company at the conclusion of the play, the leaders of Naples and Milan are "astonished at the uncouth form and savage appearance of this ugly monster" (12). In Shakespeare's *The Tempest*, Trinculo speculates on the wonder and profit displaying Caliban would produce in England (2.2.25–35), but in the Lambs' version he loses his humanity, along with any potential for ambition or authority, and is reduced to a spectacle for holiday-fools without ever leaving the island.

Without a powerful or perceptive Caliban, the Lambs are forced to eliminate all of the comic clowning and plotting of Stephano and Trin-

culo. These two characters are cut entirely. Similarly, the Lambs remove
every reference to Sebastian from the play. In their *Tempest* there is no
new vengeance, only the residue of the treachery that transpired
twelve years before. In Shakespeare's *Tempest*, Ariel reports to Prospero
that "The King, / His brother, and yours, abide all three distracted" and
are a sight that would bring pity to a human eye (5.1. 11–12). The
word *distracted* clearly connotes distress, but beyond that vague meaning the term is further open to multiple interpretations. The distracted
noblemen may be racked with guilt, teetering on the border of insanity, or simply furious after surviving a shipwreck, receiving a visit from
a harpy, and, finally, discovering themselves immobilized by an inexplicable spell. The Lambs resolve the ambiguity of Ariel's report, however, in a fashion that further diminishes the theme of vengeance in order to amplify the idea of mercy and forgiveness. The Lambs' tale says,

> The King of Naples, and Antonio the false brother, repented the in-
> justice they had done to Prospero; and Ariel told his master he was
> certain their penitence was sincere, and that he, though a spirit, could
> not but pity them. (10)

Later, the Lambs press their interpretation of the play even further by
adding a narrative description of Antonio's remorseful apology; "Antonio with tears, and sad words of sorrow and true repentance implored
his brother's forgiveness" (11). Although an actor might well choose
postures and gestures that indicate repentance in a performance of
Shakespeare's text, the original play never gives Antonio the opportunity to articulate an apology. Once he is reunited with Prospero, Shakespeare's Antonio becomes notably silent. His only line in the concluding act of the play is in response to Sebastian and describes his own
reaction to Caliban: "Very like. One of them / is a plain fish, and no
doubt marketable" (5.1.264–65). If anything, Antonio's words suggest
he remains unregenerate at the play's close, since he is already looking
about for, or at least noting, new ways to make money (by selling Caliban as a slave or side show freak) now that he has lost control of Milan.
The Lambs explain Antonio's silence very differently, "These kind words
which Prospero spoke, meaning to comfort his brother, so filled Antonio with shame and remorse, that he wept and was unable to speak"
(11–12).

The Lambs' choices in their rendition of *The Tempest* simplify the
ethical complexity of Shakespeare's text. They construct a Prospero free
from any hint of cruelty, tyranny, or repression, and erase any shadows
of lingering malice, ambition, or hostility from their villain, Antonio.
The play becomes a reassuring fable of the triumph of good over evil
and the farsighted wisdom of conventional authorities—both fathers
and kings. The Lambs' version of Shakespeare perhaps reveals less to
children of "what Shakespeare is about" and more, perhaps, of what

some adults "would like Shakespeare to be about." Close readings of the other adaptations of *The Tempest* by writers like Nesbit, Chute, Garfield, Birch, Escott, and Beneduce reveal similar authorial decisions about the place of authority and the location of blame among the play's characters. Readers examining any of these texts might consider the following questions:

- How is magic treated? Is it a legitimate form of power or a demonic force that must be vanquished?
- How is Miranda characterized? Is she dutiful or rebellious? Is she a passive or an active young woman?
- How is Caliban characterized? Is he a monstrous malignancy or an abused aboriginal or something else entirely?
- How is the relationship between Prospero and Ariel characterized? How much affection or enmity do the two share?
- How large a role do Stephano and Trinculo have in the text? What do these characters add to Shakespeare's play? Why might an adult writer be tempted to reduce, modify, or eliminate them in an adaptation for young readers?
- How is Antonio portrayed? Does he change or develop in the story? Are these changes true to Shakespeare's play?
- How significant is Ferdinand? Has his role been condensed or changed? Why and to what effect?
- How does the time period in which this version was written seem to have affected the choices made by the author?

Comparing the way the editions for young readers treat these issues with the way Shakespeare presents them will help reveal both the ambiguous complexities of the original drama and the conservative choices made by many of the adapters.

Adult fans of Shakespeare frequently express skepticism toward the premise that young adult novels might offer readers meaningful windows through which to view and interpret Shakespeare. Understandably, many people believe that the farther one moves from Shakespeare's words, the farther one moves from all that is best in his plays. Obviously, there is some merit in this argument—Shakespeare's poetry has no substitutes. Yet, the briefest comparison of Shakespearean *editions* to Shakespearean *revisions* shows that weaving Shakespeare into a new tale is often a truer form of flattery and a better indication of insight than retelling a play in simpler or more current language.

The Lambs along with the authors of all the other editions quoted in the opening of this chapter tend to present reductive simplifications of *The Tempest*. We cannot know what Shakespeare intended to say in

The Tempest, or any other play, and chasing after an author's true meaning is never any more than a game of tag with our own shadows, but we can be sure that Shakespeare wanted his play to be successful with his audiences. And neither Renaissance nor modern audiences show much enthusiasm for moralistic or didactic entertainments. We like to see good triumph over evil, but we also like to be challenged and surprised. Shakespeare is good at surprising us, a fact many editions of the plays seem to work to hide. Young adult novelists, however, generally like surprises and challenges—just as much as Shakespeare. In approaching Shakespeare's plays with the eyes of fellow writers rather than humble supplicants, they revel in the ambiguities and complexities of his plots and characters.

Like adult literary critics, who have in recent years struggled to reconsider the power and the position of Prospero—especially through the lens provided by new historicism and post-colonialism, young adult authors like Madeline L'Engle, Zibby Oneal, Tad Williams, and Dennis Covington have also brought modern insights to their readings of *The Tempest.* One of the ways these authors examine questions of authority, especially Prospero's, is by highlighting the experience of the young adults in the play—Miranda, Caliban, and Ferdinand.

Ironing Out the Wrinkles

Having won the Newbery Medal, Madeline L'Engle's *A Wrinkle in Time* (1962) has assumed a canonical status that increases the likelihood young adult readers may already be familiar with it long before they begin to read Shakespeare. Looking back at it provides both a pleasant sense of nostalgia for many readers and a kind of epiphany as well. Suddenly the Shakespearean allusions—mostly to *The Tempest,* but a few to *Hamlet* and *Macbeth*— make sense! A whole new dimension of meaning opens up before the reader. Many readers find a whole new vision of Miranda, and one much more appealing to modern sensibilities appears as well.

Shakespeare's play focuses on Prospero's return from an island exile to place and power in Milan. His daughter's education seems to provide him with a purpose during the twelve years of his absence from his kingdom. Her marriage provides him with a tool for regaining his position, a role she readily accepts. L'Engle's novel concentrates on Miranda and explores the consequences a modern young woman might face were she to invest her father with absolute power and unquestioned obedience like Shakespeare's heroine.

Meg Murry, the novel's Miranda, is a young adult consumed with self-doubt and self-loathing. Her awkward appearance, her stubborn individualism, and her unconventional family prevent her from blending smoothly into the middle-school social network. Meg particularly misses her father, a theoretical physicist (the twentieth century equivalent of a magician) whose secret work for the government has taken him away for the past two years from his family. Aided by a trio of extraterrestrials, Meg, her brother Charles Wallace, and her prospective boyfriend Calvin set off on a series of adventures crossing time and space to find Mr. Murry. Shakespeare's Miranda is central to Prospero's rescue from the island, a debt never acknowledged in the play. L'Engle's Meg discovers her father needs help to return to his home and gets full credit for aiding in his rescue.

Meg steels herself against fear and adversity during her adventure by believing in her father and his ability to fix everything, "to make it all right" (153). The extraterrestrials, whose mastery of English is shaky and who frequently rely on famous quotations to convey their ideas, use hints wrapped in Shakespearean verse to guide the adventurers. Like Ariel in *The Tempest*, Mr. Murry can be found in a "cloven pine; within which rift / Imprisoned he didst painfully remain" (101). The clue leads Meg and her companions to a transparent column where Mr. Murry stands frozen like a ragged, shipwrecked sailor (145). Meg rejoices in her reunion with her father:

> This was the moment that meant that now and forever everything would be all right. As she pressed against her father all was forgotten except joy. There was only the peace and comfort of leaning against him, the wonder of the protecting circle of his arms, the feeling of complete reassurance and safety that his presence always gave her. (149)

But her exuberance turns almost immediately to devastation when she realizes her father does not have a solution to their dilemma—he does not even know the way home;

> her father had been found but he had not made everything all right . . .
> her adored father was bearded and thin and white and not omnipo-
> tent after all. No matter what happened next, things could be no more
> terrible or frightening than they already were. (158)

Meg's father can help the adventurers, perhaps even lead them, but he cannot save them—especially from themselves. Despite his moral, intellectual, and emotional strength, he too is flawed and limited. L'Engle's young Miranda longs futilely for an all-powerful Prospero to govern and protect her.

Like many traditional interpretations of *The Tempest*, L'Engle envisions her Prospero, Mr. Murry, as a benign magician. L'Engle subverts traditional interpretations, however, by suggesting that dreams of benign omnipotence are childish. L'Engle's Prospero figure is not a tyrant or a despot, but those who seek to imbue him with omnipotence must, perforce, give up their own power of self-determination and run the risk of creating or enabling a tyrant. In order to mature, Meg has to learn to see her father as a flawed human being and to take the responsibilities, and thus the risks, of her own independence. In this version of *The Tempest*, it is Miranda, not Prospero, who must abjure magic—specifically the magical innocence and faith of childhood.

L'Engle enables Meg to make this developmental leap by providing her with a villain against which to measure her father. In Shakespeare's play, Miranda lives in a world virtually created by her father; Prospero teaches her all she knows. With his ability to rule the seas and to invoke everything from music to visions through the aid of the invisible Ariel, Miranda may, quite reasonably, see him as omnipotent. Yet, Prospero can and has erred; a combination of his own inattention to the kingdom and his ambitious brother's intrigues led to exile on the island, but these mistakes happened when Miranda was only an infant. She never has the opportunity to experience her father as a mortal, only as an all-powerful magician. Even Miranda's rebellion, her desire to befriend Ferdinand against Prospero's wishes, is really an act of unwitting obedience. Prospero arranges Miranda's encounters with Ferdinand and fabricates doubts about the young man's intentions to inspire her love. If he were a police officer, his methods would be labeled entrapment.

Unlike Miranda, however, Meg Murry gets the opportunity to see her father falter. On the dark planet Camazotz (a parody of the utopian Camelot), a disembodied brain named It rules a world of perfect order and complete stability. All individuality and idiosyncrasy is suppressed in the name of complete equality. The horrors of this regime are immediately apparent to Meg, but only slowly does it dawn on her that demanding her father provide all the answers, all the ideas, and all the resolutions to her problems only re-creates, on a personal level, the type of repression and censorship under which the inhabitants of Camazotz suffer. Independence and freedom come from embracing faults, her own and those of others, and extending and receiving love despite imperfection.

Shakespeare's Miranda grows up on an island as a result of Prospero's arrogance. She never recognizes the limitations of her circumstances, perhaps in part because Prospero tells her:

> and here
> Have I, thy schoolmaster, made thee more profit
> Than other princes can that have more time
> For vainer hours, and tutors not so careful. (1.2.171–74)

L'Engle lets her heroine begin with a belief in an omnipotent father but challenges Meg, and the novel's readers, to consider the limitations of authority, even parental authority. Whereas Shakespeare's play most often invites interpretations that maintain the patriarchal status quo, L'Engle's novel invites readers to challenge tyranny and value self-determination.

The Tempest in a New Light

Zibby Oneal's reinterpretation of *The Tempest* in her novel *In Summer Light* (1985) interrogates Shakespeare's play much more forcefully and thoroughly than L'Engle's work. Like L'Engle, Oneal makes Miranda her protagonist. Her decision to call her Kate, a name also used by Shakespeare for his most famously feisty heroine in *The Taming of the Shrew*, seems unlikely to be purely coincidental. Seventeen-year-old Kate Brewer returns to her island home for a summer of recuperation following a bout with mono. In addition to giving up a glamorous resort job, Kate must spend the summer completing a school paper on *The Tempest*. As she wrestles with the play, Kate discovers her hostility toward Prospero stems from recognition. He reminds her of her father, the famous painter Marcus Brewer. In *A Wrinkle in Time*, L'Engle challenges her Miranda to embrace independence without ever criticizing Prospero; Meg's desire to submit herself to her father's authority is a function of youthful immaturity and nothing else. Oneal's novel suggests that self-abnegating female submission stems from male arrogance and fear.

Kate's work on her Shakespeare paper is pleasantly interrupted by a growing friendship with Ian Jackson, a Berkeley graduate student spending the summer developing a retrospective of the famous painter's work. Ian greatly appreciates Marcus Brewer's accomplishments, to Kate's frustration, but he also encourages Kate to do her own painting. Although her work had won awards, her father never acknowledged it, and several years earlier the unspoken competition between Kate and her father had finally become unbearable to her. Throughout the summer Kate experiments with a return to painting, and these experiments are mirrored in her explorations of Shakespeare's Prospero:

> She wondered whether Shakespeare had ever lived on a real island, or had only imagined one. She wondered what he meant Prospero to represent. In class, some people had said he was meant to represent the artist, creating illusion from reality. Others had said, no, the whole play was meant to be political. And then, of course, there was Leah's version—the sweet, white-haired old magician, and who cared what else he might represent. (85)

Life imitates art and art imitates life for Kate—the more she thinks about her father, whom a friend even calls "magic," the better she understands Prospero. The more she thinks about art, the better she understands Marcus Brewer's power.

As the summer passes, Kate returns to her painting and falls in love with Ian. He serves as a version of Ferdinand. But just as she does with her Miranda figure, Oneal invests her Ferdinand with a greater sense of independence. Prospero sets Miranda before Ferdinand like bait in a trap, and Ferdinand eagerly steps into the snare. Unlike *The Tempest*, Oneal's book does not reinscribe the patriarchal order in its conclusion. Ian, unlike Miranda 's Ferdinand, refuses Kate, at least for now; and Kate turns instead to a perfection of her art. Rather than taking a husband, this Miranda inherits her father's talents, and insists, despite his discouragement, on practicing them. Instead, however, of painting light and landscapes, her father's specialties, Kate turns to portraits; she wants the world of her art warmed by human contact. She takes the best her father has to offer and then goes on to improve upon it in her own ways.

At the end of the summer Kate completes her essay on *The Tempest*:

> "It is wrong," she had written, "Morally, politically, humanly wrong for a ruler to ignore the need of his people. To use others for his own purposes with no concern for the cost to them is unforgivable. Prospero is guilty of these things."
>
> She had meant to end the paper there, with this indictment . . . but she hesitated. . . . "And yet at the end of the play," she wrote, "Prospero has become an old man. His magic powers are nearly gone, and then they are gone entirely. In the Epilogue he asks us to set him free. I think Shakespeare means for us to forgive him. I think he means that if we refuse, we will be trapped like Prospero was, on his island."
>
> Kate read this over. In a way it messed up her conclusion, her neat case. She wasn't even sure it was true. Maybe Shakespeare meant no such thing. But it was what she meant, so she left it. (146)

Kate learns to forgive Prospero and her father at the end of the novel, but her forgiveness is not to be mistaken for capitulation. Kate no longer bows to the male artist; at the end of her essay she abandons her attempt to interpret Shakespeare's intent and concludes with her own opinion. She imbues the play with her own meanings. Kate moves from being a dependent student to an independent thinker—she lets Shakespeare's text shape her interpretations, but she does not let it limit her ideas.

Shakespeare's Miranda grows up without a mother. Meg in *A Wrinkle in Time* has a very warm and attractive mother, but since she is absent for all the crucial action of the novel, Mrs. Murry seems almost as unimportant as Miranda's completely absent mother. Oneal supplies her Miranda with both parents, although Kate's mother does remain curiously silent through most of the book. At the end of the novel, Kate talks with her mother and makes another discovery. Although she has always known that her mother was many years ago an artist, Kate has always associated her own talent with her father. Talking with her mother about her childhood Kate suddenly has an epiphany. She realizes, "It was you who bought me the paints wasn't it? You got him to take me with him when he went to the museum Sunday afternoons" (151). Oneal's reason for restoring the mother's role in her version of *The Tempest* instantly makes sense—very impressively. Kate recognizes that while the power, the talent, may come from her father, she might never have discovered or appreciated it without her mother. In this version of *The Tempest* it seems that Mom, not Prospero, was responsible for throwing Miranda into the lifeboat as it sailed away from Milan toward the artist's magical island; the mother may still be left behind, her own artistic talent sacrificed to the genius' greater need, but she ensures her daughter's talents are not.

Unlike Prospero, Marcus Brewer never abjures his powers, but Kate, this story's Miranda, has come into her own which, among other things, enables her to see the limits of her father's art. This Prospero doesn't need to renounce his magic because it isn't really working any longer—this Miranda has broken the enchantments herself. In the final paragraphs of the novel, Kate catches the ferry to enjoy another semester at school and leaves the island behind; "and then they were too far out from land to mark details. The island floated, drifting in the sunlight, fading into the middle distance as the ferry moved on" (152). A newly empowered Kate leaves the confines of the magician's kingdom to practice her own magic, to enter a brave new world.

Defending Caliban

In addition to rethinking Miranda's relationship with Prospero, modern scholars and audiences of the play frequently ask different questions about Caliban than did Renaissance audiences. Perhaps no Shakespearean figure has appeared more variously than this island "monster." Is he, as Prospero tells us, an ungrateful and rapacious beast or is he a "natural" child untainted by the prejudices, manners, and taboos of Western civilization? Has Caliban made unwelcome sexual advances upon Miranda or is his interest in her unacceptable only to her father? Is he the recipient of Prospero's kindness or the victim of his colonial impulses? Should Caliban be considered the owner of the island or one of Prospero's subjects? Can he be all these things at once? Tad Williams presents one set of answers to these questions in *Caliban's Hour* (1994).

In Naples one night, a shape, darker even than the shadows, slips into the castle of Ferdinand and makes his way to Miranda's bedchamber. He is Caliban, after twenty years of lonely imprisonment on the island, finally escaping to wreak revenge on those who betrayed him. But Prospero is five years dead, and only Miranda remains to hear his tale and pay penance for his pain. Throughout the long hours of the night Caliban recounts to his terrified victim his version of events—his mute childhood with his mother Sycorax, his lonely youth after her death, his trepidation at the arrival of the shipwrecked magician and child, his gradual joy in joining their family, his devoted love for the maiden Miranda, his terrible disappointment when she betrays his secrets, and his painful slavery to Prospero.

Williams shapes his character from the fragments of Caliban's history narrated in Shakespeare's *The Tempest* richly augmented and reinterpreted from the perspective of an ill-treated and vengeful modern consciousness. Although uneducated when Prospero arrives on the island, Williams' Caliban is imbued with an innate sense of equity and justice. When he gradually discovers that Prospero desires him as a servant rather than a companion, his joy turns to bitter hate. When he discovers that Miranda—who is herself treated with a patriarchal blend of respect, condescension, and tyranny by Prospero—prefers to accept her father's authority and protection rather than rebel with Caliban, he is dealt a lasting emotional blow.

Shakespeare's original language makes a very scant appearance in this revision of *The Tempest* tale. Occasionally, echoes of Shakespeare's words appear edgily rewritten or placed in the mouth of a different character. This technique successfully reminds readers how often two people can honestly remember an event differently. For example, Ariel's famous song, which begins in Shakespeare with the lines:

Where the bee sucks, there suck I,
In a cowslip's bell I lie; (5.1.88–89)

becomes in Caliban's mouth:

Suck, bee; wasp sting.
Make a home for everything. (157)

What readers are accustomed to thinking of as lovely or poetic becomes ominous and ugly.

Arguably, all of Shakespeare's characters appear less attractive and likeable in Williams' revision. Prospero's ambiguous rule is reduced to a cruel and calculating tyranny. A sandy body washes up on the shore and a "waxy corpse" dangles from the rigging of the ship after the storm. This Prospero did not protect the mariners from the violence of the storm he invoked. Williams also starkly underlines the absolute and incomprehensible inhumanity of Ariel. Taking the form of a slight child, this Ariel appears without sexual characteristics, even nipples or a belly button. Ariel wracks Caliban with painful tortures not only at Prospero's bidding, but simply as a form of amusement. Ferdinand becomes, "a boy with a face pale as goat's milk, and an expression no cleverer than would adorn a goat's front" (171). Even Caliban seems diminished in some ways in this tale—his lonely plight is sympathetically illuminated, but his vengeful anger is similarly developed and expanded. He becomes more of a character, but still seems rather one-dimensional.

Unfortunately, Williams' book lacks any interesting literary qualities, and, in fact, the amateur illustrations, which accompany it, detract from, rather than enhance, the text. Caliban's monologue makes up most of the volume. The absence of dialogue, a narrator's interpreting perspective, or even some genuine self-reflection on Caliban's part is sorely missed. Sympathy for the entrapped Miranda is also hard to muster since her character lacks any compelling development. Nonetheless, the intertextual comparison the book invites may well appeal to students familiar with Shakespeare's *The Tempest*. *Caliban's Hour* enables readers to consider the events of *The Tempest* from a different point of view. The well-known aphorism that "winners write the history books" is transformed from a cliché into a genuine insight by Williams' book. Readers familiar with *The Tempest* may wonder who is ultimately more heroic or more flawed—Shakespeare's Prospero or Williams' Caliban? How does each character appeal to readers and repel them? How does Prospero's renunciation of magic in Act 5 of the play compare with Caliban's renunciation of murder in the final pages of Williams' novel? Williams' one significant addition to Shakespeare's cast, Giulietta, the daughter of Miranda and Ferdinand, also provokes questions. Is she the new servant and the new sacrifice, merely Williams' replacement for Caliban, or is Giulietta something else? How empowered is a heroine forced to choose between marriage with a distasteful man or one with an unknown stranger? Is she like Juliet eloping with the forbidden stranger or like Desdemona eloping with the strangely forbidden— both relationships doomed to self-destruct? Will running away with Caliban bring her freedom and independence or has Caliban really only become Prospero at long last—an invader laying claim to whatever he can reach? Unfortunately, *Caliban's Hour* raises many more questions than it answers. As a substitution for Shakespeare's vision, Williams' falls far short, but readers willing to explore the differences between Shakespeare's vision and Williams' will almost certainly come away with new insights into the possibilities of *The Tempest*.

A Contemporary Caliban

Dennis Covington's novel *Lizard* (1991) explores the exploitation, the denigration, and the desire for self-determination of the social outcast in his creation of a modern Caliban. Whereas Williams' sets his book in Renaissance Italy, Covington's story takes place in Louisiana and Alabama in the early 1980s. His young adult novel, winner of the Delacorte Prize, can only be considered a stunning success. Covington creatively weaves elements of Shakespeare's plot, characters, and theatrical world in and out of his novel. Sometimes readers may find a one-to-one correspondence between an element in *Lizard* and an element in *The Tempest*, but more often Covington's allusions expand and explode reflecting several aspects of Shakespeare's play simultaneously. More than any of the other young adult authors who have worked with *The Tempest*, Covington uses Shakespeare's materials to create something new, not an imitation of or a response to the original, but something rich and strange.

The novel's narrator, Lucius Sims, can't help drawing attention. His eyes, seawater in color, are set unusually wide—almost on the sides of his head. His nose is flat. He limps a bit, and his back hunches. Inside, Lucius is fine, but people tend only to notice his outside. Sent to the state school for Retarded Boys, Lucius quickly wins a nickname that reflects both his strong swimming skills and his appearance—Lizard. Life at the school is hard, but perhaps little worse than were his early years living with a woman he calls Miss Cooley, above a café in Louisiana. No one shows much concern for him anywhere.

Lizard's fortunes change one day when a troop of traveling actors puts on a performance of *Treasure Island* for the boys. At first he cannot distinguish between the fictional elements of the play and reality, but after he sneaks backstage to warn Jim Hawkins that the pirate is out to get him, he suddenly recognizes that appearance does not always mirror reality. Obviously an important element for survival, this new knowledge also will lead him to self-discovery. Although the actors initially refuse his request to take him along, the next day Lizard unexpectedly receives a visit from his "father." Lizard believes his father died on an oil rig in a tempest, a hurricane; he is torn between suspicion and excitement at the news. The stranger admits that he is actually one of the actors who recently visited the school and what he really wants is to recruit Lizard to play the role of Caliban in an upcoming production of *The Tempest*. Lizard agrees to run away from the institution and join the company. Whether or not the stranger is his father remains a mystery to Lizard.

The actor is a complicated tangle of two Shakespearean characters. Although he leads the company and will play the role of Prospero in the new production, his name is Callahan. If Lizard's outer appearance reminds readers of Shakespeare's monster Caliban, it is Callahan's twisted inner motivations that seem at times reminiscent of this namesake. Lizard wants a father, at least a friend, but Callahan explains their relationship will be strictly business: "After the show and we get paid you're on your own. If you want to go back to the school, that's fine, although you don't belong there" (52). Like Prospero, Callahan seizes what he needs for his own purposes but promises Lizard will be freed to make his own choices once he has finished.

Sallie, the production's Ariel, turns out to be a more sympathetic friend to Lizard. She explains the play to him and what his role will entail. This synopsis of Shakespeare's play serves to remind readers of some of the plot elements and conflicts Covington is most interested in with his revision, but it cannot substitute for a detailed knowledge of *The Tempest.* Covington's interpretive use of the drama is far too complex and in many ways depends on a reader's ability to recall and rethink intimate elements of the relationships among Shakespeare's characters. The better a reader knows *The Tempest,* the more he or she will find in *Lizard.*

Before Callahan and Sallie can leave Louisiana and head to Birmingham, Alabama, where *The Tempest* will be staged, they have a few more performances of *Treasure Island* to complete. Left to his own devices at a rural campground while Callahan and Sallie are out, Lizard discovers two teenagers living alone in a dilapidated shack—they seem as isolated and forgotten as the island inhabitants of Shakespeare's *Tempest.* Their mother, reminiscent of Shakespeare's Sycorax, is dead. Like Caliban in the play, they claim ownership of the property based on familial inheritance and upon native due. Sammy, the younger of the two teenagers, says, "it was deeded to me by my great-great-grandfather, Chief Narrow Meadow. I'm full-blooded Creek" (58). Lizard recognizes the boy's "bald-faced lie"; his appearance reveals African American ancestry in addition to any Native American blood, but he still finds Sammy and his sister, Rain, entrancing. Sammy is a kind of Ariel; he claims to know magic and, at least initially, treats Lizard poorly, referring to him as a "subhuman, humpbacked thing" (59). Rain plays Miranda. Her name functions as an anagram of the opening letters used for Shakespeare's heroine, and they are both fifteen years old. She takes on elements of Shakespeare's Caliban, too. In *The Tempest* Caliban claims to have shown Prospero and Miranda "all the qualities o' th' isle, / The fresh springs, brine pits, barren place, and fertile" (1.2.340–41). In the novel Rain plays host to Lizard and shows him all the qualities of her home. She gives him food, offers him water, and shows him their secret cave. Rain also responds to his desperate need for friendship and affection. Covington seems at times even to hint at the potential for romance between the two.

Rain and Sammy do not, however, live in complete isolation. They are visited occasionally by Preacher, a version of Prospero. He treats Sammy and Rain abusively, but they don't know how to escape him. Sammy explains:

He's not really a preacher. He just claims to be. He was Mama's boyfriend a long time ago, and he says he's got the papers to show that we
belong to him. Even though we live in town, he's what they call a
guardian." (72)

Preacher may not be a magician like Prospero, but his legal claims on
the young adults give him a great deal of power over the siblings; their
lack of money or other resources to contest his treatment makes his
power virtually unlimited. Once Lizard arrives, the cast is complete.
Shakespeare's Prospero, Caliban, Miranda, and Ariel are paralleled in
tangled ways by Covington's Preacher, Lizard, Rain, and Sammy. Although, Lizard is forced to leave his new friends to travel with Callahan
and Sallie, he doesn't forget them. Just as Shakespeare's play includes
a subplot with Trinculo, Stephano, and Caliban struggling to overthrow
Prospero, a secondary plot line in Covington's novel follows Lizard's
struggles to free Rain and Sammy from their enslavement to Preacher.
Shakespeare's audiences tend to root for Prospero; Covington subver-
sively invites readers to side with the rebels.

Once Lizard arrives in Birmingham, he is introduced to the South-
side Repertory Company's proprietor, Waldo Stakes, whose initials
echo those of another famous theater personage, William Shakespeare.
Callahan doesn't like what he finds; the company is not well organized. The repertory season hasn't been set; there is no money to pay
the actors; nothing beyond the first night's performance of *The Tempest*
is established. The fortunes of the actors will rise or fall based on a
single performance. To a modern actor such conditions seem hideous,
but these are the exact conditions under which Renaissance plays pre-
miered, especially when performed by traveling companies.

Sallie begins to work with Lizard on his lines. At first he can hardly
understand a word of Shakespeare's dialogue. Eventually he begins to
find meaning and an identity in the play:

> I was Caliban. I lived alone on the island my mother had given me un-
> til this magician Prospero and his daughter Miranda washed up on the
> beach one day. . . . I was supposed to be mad at Prospero, mad enough
> to kill him. The words came out the way they were in the script be-
> cause I memorized them exactly that way, but the meaning was some-
> thing else, something in my head. (119)

As his rehearsals intensify, Lizard's relationship with Callahan deterio-
rates. Callahan drinks too much, he flirts with women besides Sallie, and
he teases Lizard with tantalizing bits of information about his family. In
these scenes Callahan seems to take on some of the aspects of Shakespeare's Ariel. Callahan even pinches Lizard under the table in the bar,
just as Ariel torments Caliban pinching him with unseen fingers.

When he isn't in rehearsals, Lizard works to help Rain and Sammy. Before he left, Rain gave him a silver bowl, a family relic. She instructs him to sell it, and send the money to their Aunt Eunice. She can use it to come rescue them. Sallie suggests Lizard take the bowl to a museum to be appraised. There he meets another small set of minor characters who once again echo Shakespeare's cast. In his chapter on "Intertextualities" in the third volume of *Adolescent Literature as a Complement to the Classics* (1996), John Noell Moore points out how the curator of the museum, Mr. Robert Howell, works as a benevolent Prospero while the janitor and sculptor, William Tyson, serves as a version of Ariel (81). The bowl is a disappointment; it isn't silver at all, only a leaded-glass knickknack. Lizard learns he can't rely on a magic talisman to save his friends. He will have to look for a solution himself.

On the opening night of *The Tempest,* Lizard fears he will throw up, but Callahan is the one who fumbles once they all get on stage. When Lizard looks into his eyes, he sees a man even more defenseless and terrified than he is himself. Lizard seems, simultaneously, to discover the truth about Callahan and Prospero—neither man is as powerful as he pretends. The knowledge sets Lizard free—free of his fear and free of Shakespeare's language. The lines that pour out of his mouth are not the words he memorized, but his understanding of them:

> "In payment I took you all over the island. . . . And soon I even knew words for things I'd never seen. Like love. . . . But the words tumbled around in my head" I paused. "I could think, but I didn't know whether thinking was a gift or a curse. For all I could think about was love. . . . I'd lost my kingdom for love," I said, stepping toward him across the sand. "And what good was the knowledge you'd given in return? What good was knowing the word for love without knowing the thing?" (141)

To Lizard's surprise, this intense and personal moment on stage helps heal his relationship with Callahan, and an odd but meaningful chemistry develops between the two actors on stage and off.

The local reviews attack much of the production, but Lizard's performance gets singled out because of his "beautifully grotesque mask." Life and art, appearance and reality have become inextricably entwined. Lizard only finds the truth about his relationship with Callahan on stage, and the reviewer looks at the stage and mistakes the actor's real appearance for the character's costume. Instead of becoming more distinct, actors and characters fuse even more deeply and complexly as the novel progresses.

After the production ends, Waldo Stakes offers Lizard a home—he could become one of "Shakespeare's children," but instead he chooses to return to Louisiana with Callahan; he wants to help Rain and Sammy.

They find the shack deserted. Soon, they learn Preacher is on trial for murdering a black female. Lizard takes Rain's death hard, but he goes to the trial anyway. As with so many of the deaths in *The Tempest*, this one is only an illusion. Rain and Sammy are at the trial too. Deep in their secret cave, Sammy discovered bones, the bones of their long absent mother. Preacher murdered her. In Covington's version of *The Tempest*, Sycorax still ruled the "island" when Prospero arrived; he had to murder to take control of the kingdom. Confronting Preacher with the truth of his behavior leads eventually to freedom for Rain and Sammy.

Lizard and Rain make plans to meet again at the local fair in the fall. Rain and Sammy find a home with Aunt Eunice. Lizard lets Callahan take him home to Miss Cooley, the woman who raised him; this time she puts him in public school, not a state institution. At the end of Shakespeare's play Prospero takes responsibility for Caliban. He tells the other characters, "This thing of darkness, I / Acknowledge mine" (5.1.278–79). Audiences are left to ponder whether he is speaking symbolically or literally. At the end of the novel, Miss Cooley finally acknowledges Lizard as her son. Lizard also finally realizes that Callahan isn't his father, though he still hates to see him leave. Like Prospero, Callahan disappears without saying goodbye and only writes Lizard a letter to let him know he "never meant any harm" (197). The novel ends as ambiguously as the play. One set of loose ends have been tied up; they have all made peace with the past. The future of the characters, however, still stretches out in front of them; they have all embarked on new lives.

Due to the odd physical arrangement of his eyes, Lucius Sims is forced to look at things with, "first one eye and then the other"(6). Covington asks his readers to do the same thing. His novel invites complex interpretations. On its own, *Lizard* introduces striking explorations of identity and community. Paired with Shakespeare's drama the levels of meaning and allusion grow even richer. Various and varied echoes and reflections of Caliban, Miranda, Ariel, and Prospero appear throughout the novel. With one eye turned to *The Tempest* and the other turned to *Lizard,* readers, like Lucius, see everything from a new and unique perspective.

A Tempest of Conclusions

Romantic, parental, racial, and political conflicts all have significance for modern readers, and *The Tempest* offers plenty of material in each of these areas. One of the primary differences between writers who create editions of *The Tempest* and those who create novelistic revisions of the play comes in their approach to conflict. The Lambs and those who followed in their footsteps preparing editions of the tales for young readers tend to ignore, simplify, or remove conflict from the drama. L'Engle, Oneal, Williams, and Covington, conversely, focus on one or more of these conflicts.

Modern attitudes toward conflict are very complex and fragmented. We often seem to flee it in fear forgetting that conflict itself is not dangerous (or avoidable); it is the methods used to resolve conflict that must be considered with care. In some ways, L'Engle and Williams protect themselves, or maybe their readers, from the dangers of conflicts by setting their novels in fantasy worlds. L'Engle's dystopian world of Camazotz and Williams' historically distant Renaissance Italy enable readers to think about the conflicts in the play without being faced with the realities of them. Oneal and Covington courageously set their novels in contemporary America. They ask readers to look both at the conflicts embedded in *The Tempest* and the conflicts resulting from growing up. In many ways, they bring us closer to the play by bringing it into our world instead of asking us to make an imaginative leap toward another world.

My explications of these editions and revisions of *The Tempest* are not intended to be conclusive, but merely suggestive of the allusive richness to be found in various treatments of Shakespeare's work. As modern readers examine the play and these texts, more levels of meaning are sure to unfold. Every writer who takes on *The Tempest* brings something new and individual to the play, and so, of course, does every reader. And the more versions of *The Tempest* a reader explores, the richer the intertextualities will become. For example, Shakespeare's Caliban can be put into conversation not just with Williams' or Covington's or the Lambs' characters, but all four together. In the world of young adult literature, fine old tales expand and welcome many brave new people.

Chapter Eight

Othello and *The Merchant of Venice*: Challenging the Status Quo

Despite the fact that Shakespeare wrote nearly forty plays (the exact number depends on whether or not his collaborations with another playwright named Fletcher are numbered in the tally), the standard curriculum of American schools rarely admits to the existence of more than *Romeo and Juliet, Macbeth, Hamlet, Julius Caesar,* and *King Lear.* Schools with the resources to offer a special class in Shakespeare may offer a small number of their students a greater variety of plays, but more often than not, class study is limited to a selection of these five tragedies. In part this stranglehold on the curriculum is an effect of large textbook conglomerates that choose to feature the same old chestnuts in nationally distributed volumes year after year. In part it is an effect of "Shakesfear;" teachers uncomfortable with the complexities of Renaissance drama teach and reteach only those few plays that they themselves were taught. In part it is a lingering echo of Puritan reproach left over from the days when anything smacking of sexuality was considered inappropriate for the classroom; the tragedies revel more in carnage than the carnal.

Given the wide range of topics addressed in Shakespeare's works, the plays most often taught in schools comprise a very peculiar list. *Romeo and Juliet* transforms two lovers who value impulsive actions over thoughtful decisions, self-determination over adult guidance, and pessimistic self-destruction over optimistic determination into heroes. Sure, Shakespeare eventually destroys Romeo and Juliet, but only to demonstrate the failures of the adult community. Any adolescent who has ever considered suicide in order "to make them all sorry" has a fine pair of role models in the illustrious young lovers. *Hamlet,* on the other hand, tells the tale of a young man who dislikes his stepfather, and who prefers to pout, rhapsodize about suicide, and lash out at his mother, girlfriend, and buddies rather than directly confront the object of his disdain. In the end, he explodes with pent-up frustration and kills his stepfather, losing his own life in the process as well. *Julius Caesar* takes on the problem of betrayal. Brutus gives into peer pressure and knifes his best friend; isn't it always better to be one of the "in crowd" than risk the dangers of ostracism and ridicule by standing up for your friends? But enough with the sarcasm . . . all of Shakespeare's plays have plenty of meat for both praise and censure.

Fortunately, publishers continue to bring out inexpensive volumes of the plays enabling many teachers to purchase a class set of *Twelfth Night* instead of being restricted to the tragedy printed in the sophomore literature anthology. (Dover Press deserves particular accolades in this arena for making basic versions of many of the plays available for only one dollar a copy!) Well-designed classroom guides like the Folger Library's *Shakespeare Set Free* series edited by Peggy O'Brien (1993– 1995), among many others, encourage teachers to experiment with new plays and new teaching methods. A spurt of recent film productions, from the Academy Award winning *Shakespeare in Love* (1998) to the traditional *A Midsummer's Night Dream* (1999) to the radically revised *Ten Things I Hate About You* (1999), is working to make Shakespeare both culturally visible and surprisingly popular. Some of these other texts, especially *Othello* and *The Merchant of Venice,* seem to offer particularly compelling material for today's readers.

Othello's Appeal

Othello is not among the Shakespearean texts most frequently taught in classrooms. The play raises difficult questions about racism and stereotyping. Some people feel that to teach the text is to acquiesce to the worst values in the play. But if this is the case, then a large number of other Shakespearean plays need to be reconsidered too; women, Jews, the French, and the poor, among others, are all derided, sometimes vigorously, in Shakespeare's plays.

Rather than justifying or sanctioning racism, *Othello* provides wonderful opportunities for exploring its complexities. For example, Shakespeare uses the images of color in ways that help clarify how racial self-consciousness, if not racism itself, is intertwined into our very language. When Iago explains to Desdemona's father that "an old black ram is tupping your white ewe" (1.1.88–89) in the opening scene of the play, his warning is as much about race as it is about an unsanctioned sexual encounter. Stereotyping is also rampant in the play. Some of the attributes associated with Othello, at least in part due to his racial background, may seem benign, or even appealing. His strength and experience as a warrior are envied and employed by the Venetians to bolster their own military. But when Othello grows jealous of Desdemona's friendship with Cassio, these characteristics are quickly subverted into cruelty and cunning. The narrow view of human nature that allows the Venetians initially to view Othello as a military tool rather than an individual are the same views that enable Iago to view him as a puppet rather than a man.

Othello, too, is entrapped in the vicious cycle of racism that drives the drama. His desire to join Venetian civilization blinds him to the fact that one of the very characteristics of that civilization is a disregard for people from his culture. To become a Venetian he must, at least in part, abandon his own vision of himself as honest, adventurous, and beloved and adopt the Venetian image of himself as "a base Indian," "a malignant and turban'd Turk," and a "circumcised dog" (5.2.347, 353, 355). Once Othello begins to understand the ignoble vision of himself, he also begins to enact it. Othello begins the play by repudiating the racism of the Venetians, but the more he becomes one of them—by marrying Desdemona, governing the people of Cyprus, making friends with other Venetian officers—the more he begins to doubt himself and his own judgment. He begins to wonder how a beautiful Venetian woman could be satisfied with him or why a flamboyant young man like Cassio would choose his company. Othello's tragedy is that he succeeds in living up to other people's expectations. In *Othello* Shakespeare illustrates the insidious destruction racism brings to everyone it touches.

In his 1995 work entitled *Othello: A Novel,* Julius Lester tackles the difficulties of teaching Shakespeare's play by forefronting many of the racial conflicts in the play and representing them in the form of a young adult novel. His text seems neither a modernized edition of *Othello* nor a novelistic revision of the play's characters and themes, but rather something in between.

Othello: A Novel by Julius Lester

Shakespearean adaptations for young readers reach a new level of sophistication in the work of Julius Lester. Well established as a scholar and author of books ranging from his four collections of Uncle Remus stories to his recent adaptation of the controversial tale of Little Black Sambo, entitled *Sam and the Tigers* (1996), Lester is no stranger to the task of presenting complex ideas of race and culture to young readers.

Many of the authors working in this field furnish a list of justifications, sometimes apologetically, for adapting or tampering with Shakespeare. Lester, too, explains his desire to make Shakespeare more accessible and appealing, but unlike his predecessors, he goes on to explain and analyze some of the consequences of his project. Plays, he tells his readers in the introduction to his book, are public, collaborative events while novels are private and intimate (x). The addition of descriptions and interior monologues, features of a novel, has enabled, even forced, new questions about the characters in Shakespeare's play.

Three sets of changes Lester makes deserve the most attention. First, Lester moves Othello's story from Italy to England. He explains this decision as a simple convenience, but the change is more than superficial. Located in England, the racism of the text seems more overt. When the play is set in Italy, readers can more easily perceive the complicated racial conflicts as something "foreign." Most American readers will know better than to assume that the play stands as a mirror reflecting the behavior of real Italians, but the problems will, nonetheless, seem far away. Placing his story in England, Lester invites readers to look at racial conflicts as a part of our long history—something the first colonists brought with them to America. Yet, setting the play in England means other elements of Shakespeare's drama are lost. The major and the minor ramifications of Lester's change provide material for discussion among readers who study both versions of the play.

Lester makes an even more significant revision when he changes the race of two of the characters in Shakespeare's play—Iago and Emilia. Lester explains his decision:

> If race was going to be more central in the novel, and it was, Iago could not be white, because his jealousy might stereotype him as a racist. I found it more interesting to explore racist feelings in a black person. (xiii)

In Shakespeare's *Othello* the title character speaks, in some ways, for all outsiders. The specific race of Othello is, in some ways, actually quite insignificant. We aren't exactly sure what Shakespeare meant by the word *moor,* which is as close as he actually comes to labeling Othello with a racial designation. He may have been referring to Othello's culture, his color, or both. And, as Lester points out, Othello seems deracinated in the play—there is nothing about his language, belief systems, or behavior that are necessarily African (xii). In Shakespeare's *Othello* race or color merely serve as a visual reminder of the hero's status as an outsider. With this shift, Lester succeeds in fragmenting an all too common vision of black people as monolithic or homogeneous. There is no "black view" in this novel any more than there is a "white view." In Lester's novel there are sympathetic and offensive individuals of both races. Furthermore, envisioning Emilia and Iago as black, Lester makes space for dialogue; the three African characters can, and frequently do, discuss their opinions on issues like intermarriage, cultural loss, and immigration. Through these discussions Lester reveals complex varieties of racism demonstrating a view of racism more important to modern readers—racism is not white against black, but people against people.

Lester's third major innovation in his novel comes through his creation of a back story. He explains aspects of the characters' histories that are left open in Shakespeare's play. Readers learn how Othello came to leave his country, what sort of relationship Desdemona and Cassio had before the play began, and what happened to Desdemona's mother. Lester also resolves several issues that Shakespeare seems to leave intentionally ambiguous; for example, we learn in this novel what motivates Iago's malice. In the play, Iago gives a variety of reasons without ever really explaining his hatred. In the novel, Iago has hated Othello since the first day the two met Emilia—and she gazed with adoration upon Othello. Readers may enjoy or disdain the anwers Lester provides to many of the questions Shakespeare's play produces, but both fans and detractors will find them worthy of discussion.

In his introduction, Lester briefly discusses these three sets of changes with readers and illustrates his creative process by listing the kinds of questions he discovered himself asking as he began to transform the play into a novel:

> How did Othello get to England? How had he adjusted to life there? Did he miss his homeland? What had his homeland been like? Who had he been in his homeland? What was his name in Africa? Did he think of himself as European or African or both? (xii–xiii).

And in answering these questions Lester produces a new *Othello*—a story set in England rather than Italy, a story with three black characters rather than one, a story as much about identity as it is about jealousy. Lester explains he isn't simply "translating" Shakespeare for modern audiences, he is retelling it to forefront his own interests and questions. In doing so, Lester is not usurping Shakespeare's vision or authority, he is only following his lead. Shakespeare didn't create the story of Othello, he also borrowed it from a predecessor, probably the French translator Gabriel Chapuys, who borrowed it from the Italian poet, Giraldi Cinthio.

One of Lester's treatments of Shakespeare's text is, however, less provocative and more provoking. Direct quotations from Shakespeare's play along with close paraphrases are printed with a boldface font throughout the novel. Although this technique certainly serves as a convenience for readers wishing to draw close comparisons between

Lester's version of the tale and Shakespeare's and saves them the work of hunting down these echoes on their own, it is terribly disruptive. It is also misleading. The vast majority of Lester's tale draws on Shakespeare for inspiration. Highlighting only a few verbal parallels seems to invite foreclosure of all the other interesting ways Lester has adapted and adopted the language of his source.

Regardless of this distraction, Lester's novel is a compelling retelling of Shakespeare's *Othello*. He changes the tale thoroughly enough to make it his own without ever ignoring the source of his inspiration. Some readers will prefer it to the play. Other readers will champion Shakespeare. But the only way to tell is to read both versions!

Othello as Shakespeare

In the creatively constructed novel *Black Swan* (1993), Farrukh Dhondy takes on two terrific Shakespearean issues. On a small scale he explores the experience of the racial outsider in Renaissance England. On a larger scale he posits an intriguing, if wildly unlikely, hypothesis about the real identity of the author of the plays attributed to Shakespeare. He imagines a young black actor who, like Othello, suffers great jealousy, but who, like Shakespeare, writes plays. Dhondy's novel demands a sophisticated reader, probably one who enjoys mystery. The book intertwines three different embedded narratives taking place in two different time periods. The book's main protagonist is Rose Hassan, a talented young actress. While most of her classmates will spend the summer before beginning university studies on exciting trips, Rose knows she must find a job to help earn the money she needs to support herself in college. Her mother's sudden illness only intensifies her problems. Fortunately, her mother's employer, a mysterious recluse named Mr. Bernier, is willing to let Rose substitute as a caregiver and personal secretary until her mother recovers. He is a strange man, but the high wages he offers are too tempting for Rose to pass up. Among other tasks, Rose's employer asks her to help him transcribe the diaries of Simon Forman, a Renaissance alchemist with a love of the theater. These diaries, which chronicle Forman's involvement with various actors, writers, spies, and criminals, provide the second strand of narrative in the novel. Along with his own notes, Forman also uses his diaries to record the tale of Henry, a freed black slave struggling to make a life in the London theater. Henry's story produces the third narrative embedded in the novel.

Dhondy's novel weaves real Renaissance history with fictitious additions in complex and clever ways. Student readers of the book may enjoy exploring the real figures Dhondy adopts and transforms as much as they enjoy the novel. For example, surviving Renaissance records thoroughly document the life and interests of Simon Forman (1552–1611) who practiced astrology and medicine, often a few steps outside of legal boundaries. His excesses earned him several jail sentences during his life. From a modern perspective, Forman's work seems too dependent on superstitions and occult practices to take seriously. In his own day, however, Forman was a sort of scientist struggling to discover the laws of nature. Sometimes he strayed too far into magical practices, sometimes he took advantage of his customers, but some of his work was quite serious and helped pave the way for real scientific progress during the seventeenth century. Renaissance theater scholars have for years studied him with interest because his diaries help pinpoint the dates when some of Shakespeare's plays were written, including *Macbeth, Cymbeline,* and *The Winter's Tale,* and give an idea of how well they were received during their first performances.

Christopher Marlowe is another real Renaissance figure important in Dhondy's *Black Swan.* Marlowe has long been a figure of interest for Renaissance scholars. He was born in 1564, the same year as Shakespeare, and the careers of Marlowe and Shakespeare parallel and contradict each other in tantalizing ways. Unlike Shakespeare, Marlowe attended Cambridge University and apparently from a very young age had contacts with important government officials. He also began writing successful plays before Shakespeare; by 1587 his play *Tamburlaine* was the talk of London. He specialized in tragedies written in such powerful blank verse that his style became the standard for many years. Shakespeare was one of the many playwrights who imitated him. But Marlowe seems to have had another career in addition to the theater, spying. Records are, of course, sketchy; most governments are careful to conceal information about their spies, but adding together the evidence from a variety of sources reveals that Marlowe probably worked both in England and abroad as a secret agent. Nonetheless, Marlowe was often in trouble with the law for fighting, forgery, homosexuality, and atheism. When he died suddenly in 1593, allegedly during a fight over a bar tab, many wondered whether his death was truly accidental or an arranged murder. It is unlikely we will ever know. Scholars of Renaissance drama wonder how his art would have developed had he lived—many believe he would have rivaled Shakespeare as the premier poet of the age.

Dhondy attempts to answer these speculative questions in his novel by creating a fictional view of the Renaissance in which Marlowe doesn't die in 1593. In Dhondy's novel, Simon Forman helps Marlowe foil the assassination attempt by substituting another corpse in place of Marlowe's body in the bar. The authorities think Marlowe is dead, but instead he lives on writing plays secretly. Henry, the freed black slave, also becomes a secret author of dramas. Most of these plays are passed on to a hapless young actor named William Shakespeare who agrees to present them as his own work.

With this plot twist, Dhondy confronts the sticky issue of Shake-spearean authorship. Throughout Shakespeare's life and for more than two hundred years following it, virtually no one questioned whether the real author of Shakespeare's plays was Shakespeare. Today, as well, only a very, very few serious Shakespeare scholars see any compelling evidence that Shakespeare is not the real author of the plays. Generally, the arguments against Shakespeare's authorship are perceived to be mis-guided and poorly informed conspiracy theories. Unfortunately, usually only people who have studied the Renaissance have enough experi-ence to weed fact from fiction within these theories. Like most con-spiracy theories, those surrounding Shakespeare's authorship are fasci-nating to explore, but students should be warned against taking them seriously. In fact, the question of why some people would rather expose Shakespeare as a hoax instead of engaging with his plays may in itself be a very revealing question for readers to explore.

Only in the nineteenth century when the study of Shakespeare be-came a specialty and Shakespeare himself rose in status from a beloved artist to an English icon did questions about authorship begin to sur-face. All of the arguments against Shakespeare's authorship are cen-tered in two contentions: first, that Shakespeare lacked the education to write such complex and sophisticated dramas, and second, that Shakespeare lacked the necessary class standing to write so convincingly about kings and courtiers. At their root, both of these arguments are very elitist and antidemocratic; they insist that a person from the lower-middle classes is incapable of achieving greatness. Both arguments, however, fail to understand the social conditions of the Renaissance. While it is true that Shakespeare probably did not receive a university education, the grammar school he had the opportunity to attend in Stratford for up to ten years would have provided a fine classical educa-tion. Many of the famous artists and statesmen of the English Renais-sance received very similar educations. Those doubting Shakespeare's authorship seem to have forgotten the fact that it is only in the last few decades of Western civilization that a university education has become standard. Shakespeare's lack of court connections is also no barrier to his position as author of the plays. Although, many of the dramas do include scenes of court life, none of them include scenes of contempo-rary courtly politics. Shakespeare modeled his kings, courtiers, and military commanders on those he had read about in Latin classics, his-tory chronicles, and other plays.

Doubters of Shakespeare's authorship are forced to overlook all of the contemporary evidence that Shakespeare did have the means to write the plays and suggest, instead, some other more aristocratic can-

didate. During the nineteenth century, Francis Bacon was the most popular candidate. Recently Edward de Vere, the earl of Oxford, has been
more popular. Sometimes other candidates like Christopher Marlowe
and even Queen Elizabeth herself are put forward. In each of these
cases the conspiracy theorists need to explain why their candidate
would have gone to all the trouble to hide his or her identity and use
Shakespeare as a front man. And in each case, the conspiracy theorists
are forced to construct elaborate and unprovable hypotheses about secret motivations or conflicts to justify their candidate's alleged actions.
To any complaint that the theory "doesn't make sense," or "there isn't
any evidence for that," conspiracy theorists simply retort, "Of course,
not! They had to hide everything to keep it secret." The accusation that
Shakespeare did not write the plays is unlikely to ever disappear because the conspiracy theorists will explain any holes in their arguments as "further evidence of the conspiracy." There is no way to refute
such circular claims. On the other hand, conspiracy theorists will never
prove any of their candidates is the true author of the plays because
they have no evidence.

Nonetheless, as long as readers remember that Christopher Marlowe really did die in 1593 and that there are no records of freed black
slaves living in Elizabethan England (let alone becoming actors and
playwrights), Dhondy's novel makes a fine amusement. Of the two
characters whom Dhondy suggests as the real authors of the plays, the
works of the freed slave, Henry (who is also referred to as Lazarus), are
by far the most interesting. Dhondy explores some of the difficulties a
black man would have encountered in Renaissance England. Henry
first encounters problems after he flees a life of slavery on Hispaniola
to become a sailor on the English merchant ship The Resurrection.
Mutineers gain control of the ship, but Henry remains alive by taking
advantage of their fear. They cannot understand his curses (spoken in
his native language) and assume he has the powers of the devil. They
are afraid to kill him. When an English fleet subdues the mutineers, the
atrocities are all blamed on Henry. Henry explains how he gets framed
for the high-seas crimes:

> [they] told the tale of how I had eaten the hearts of the victims of our
> several encounters, that when we overwhelmed a ship and killed the
> crew, I would board it, cutlass in hand and dig out the hearts of the
> dying. That I was a practitioner of the dark sciences and played with
> the Devil with my arts. (66)

These lies nearly get Henry hanged, but with the help of Simon Forman, he escapes and takes up a new life and identity.

The practice of hiding his face leads Henry into the profession of
acting. On stage wearing a disguise seems natural, but he can only take
small parts. Fame might bring him unwanted recognition. Acting also

brings him into a friendship with Marlowe. For a time, Henry lives happily with Marlowe, presumably as lovers and friends. But Marlowe's own problems with the law and a need to hide his identity drive him to France and into a new relationship with another young man named Sebastian. Henry finds Marlowe's betrayal almost unbearable:

> It was as deep as Hell this hunger to know more, everything. And I had no certain knowledge that they even knew each other. Yet, and yet Christopher who had sworn so many oaths to me, who had promised to return now or send for me—God, I knew that this boy had his favor.
>
> My only proof—and how I clung to it—while wishing it wasn't true, was the pattern on the handkerchief that the boy pulled to wipe his brow at rehearsal. Did I fancy it or was he flaunting his kerchief? Was it not the one I gave Christopher . . . I would know that handkerchief and pick it out if you strewed handkerchiefs like stars before me. (182–83)

Dhondy cleverly suggests where the author of *Othello* may have found his inspiration for the handkerchief so central to the play's plot. In this novel *Othello* the Moor of Venice is firmly rooted in the experiences of the Moor of London.

Soon Henry transforms his misery into art by writing a tragic drama. Abandoning his low profile, he even takes the lead role. To his glee or his horror, Dhondy doesn't tell us, his rival, Sebastian, ends up playing Desdemona. During a climatic performance, Henry appears to kill himself on stage—art and life have become so entangled as to be indistinguishable for him; he doesn't just play Othello, he is Othello. But his body disappears and readers are left wondering if the corpse was stolen (as some gossips whispered) or if Henry has once again cheated death. In fact, readers may even wonder if the mysterious Mr. Bernier, one of the two central characters from the novel's primary story line, may not share some uncanny relationship with Henry.

Dhondy's *Black Swan,* apparently a clever reference to Shakespeare's well-known nickname of the Swan of Avon, invites readers to explore a tangled literary web that crosses fact with fiction, Renaissance settings with modern London sites, and drama with mystery. As Othello tells Desdemona when he gives her the handkerchief, many readers may find "there's magic in the web of it" (3.4.69).

Refusing Iago

A more light-hearted and simpler approach to *Othello* is embedded in Kate Gilmore's novel *Jason and the Bard* (1993). Gilmore's novel invites readers to experience the complex and exhilarating world of Shakespeare's theater through the eyes of a modern apprentice. In addition to learning about the stage, Jason also learns about the temptations of jealousy and competition.

Entranced by the promise of a summer spent submerged in Shakespeare, Jason applies for the apprentice program at the fictitious Avon Shakespeare Festival in a small college town in central Ohio. Like the other five apprentices in the program, Jason has plenty of experience with roles in school productions, but this is his first opportunity to perform with a professional company, and even more importantly, with a repertory company. During the summer season, the company will perform six different Shakespearean productions each week—*Othello, Titus Andronicus, Antony and Cleopatra, Romeo and Juliet, The Merchant of Venice,* and *The Tempest.* Although the major roles are reserved for professional actors, the apprentices are assigned many small roles. Jason finds himself scheduled for sixteen bit parts and a large understudy role, in addition to daily duties with the property manager and lessons in stage combat, Shakespearean diction, and a host of other professional skills.

As readers become involved in the extraordinarily complicated, highly organized, and exhausting sets of preparations necessary to the Avon Shakespeare Festival's success, they are simultaneously introduced to a number of production issues from both the Renaissance and the modern stage. Shakespeare's own acting company, along with the other companies of the era, was also a repertory troop. Over the course of a year, Renaissance acting companies performed literally dozens of different full-length plays. Complicating this regimen, most actors in Shakespeare's age played two or more roles in each drama. This practice, called *doubling,* was necessary since the company could usually afford only twelve to twenty-four men (the exact number varied from one season to the next and from company to company). Yet, plays had dozens of speaking roles. Both *Antony and Cleopatra* and *Richard III* have well over thirty named characters, in addition to crowds of soldiers, citizens, and servants. Acting in these companies demanded amazing flexibility and range on top of memorization skills astounding by modern standards.

As Jason helps Joe, a professional actor only a few years older than himself, learn the lines for his title role in *Othello* (along with his substantial roles in the other five plays), he develops an understanding of the difficulty and strain of the acting profession. Jason also learns to negotiate the egos of the more experienced actors, laugh patiently at the misadventures of his fellow apprentices, and anticipate the demands of the directors and technical staff—all theatrical challenges he never anticipated. Unlike Shakespeare's world, the Avon company employs women on stage, hires African American actors, and uses electricity to light the scenes instead of sunlight, but the most essential feature of the theater, the alchemy that transforms assorted individuals into a well-knit company, is timeless. Gilmore is an author who remembers that Shakespeare is drama, not simply poetry, not just beautiful words, but soaring language augmented with bloody hands, baskets of hissing asps, and ethereal music pouring out from the shadowy world beneath the stage.

Gilmore's plot goes well beyond the magic and the mechanics of the Shakespearean theater; Jason finds himself embroiled in a mysterious set of practical jokes, romantically inclined toward several of the talented and attractive female apprentices, and tested (quite ironically) when an unexpected opportunity to play the role of the tragic turn-coat Enobarbus in *Antony and Cleopatra* pits professional ambitions against hard-won friendship.

The relationships within the novel cast Jason as a sort of Iago to Joe's Othello. Like Iago, Jason seems to have little power within the hierarchy of the acting company, but his help has the potential to make or break Joe. Like Othello, Joe is a fine swordsman; he is in charge of Jason's stage combat instruction. He is generous with his time and knowledge—an open, likeable young man just reaching the pinnacle of his strength and ready for a big break in his stage career. Jason can support Joe at the expense of his own opportunity to play the important role of Enobarbus, or he can exploit his role as Joe's line coach feeding Joe's fears of inadequacy and failure instead of expelling them. Both Jason and Joe rise above their literary parallels. Jason sustains the integrity both Shakespeare's Enobarbus and Iago renounce. Joe succeeds in performing a fine Othello without falling victim to that character's infamous jealousies and insecurities. Male friendship fails the heroes of both *Antony and Cleopatra* and *Othello* but not the heroes of Gilmore's novel.

Transforming Desdemona

Just as Gilmore concentrates her novel on the potential strength of male friendship, Louise Plummer looks at how women can help each other discover the truth—in relationships and in themselves. In her novel *The Unlikely Romance of Kate Bjorkman* (1995), Plummer attempts to integrate characteristics of two very distinct Shakespearean heroines in order to create a realistic modern heroine. Desdemona stands, for many audiences, as an epitome of classic feminine virtues—she is quiet, strong, loving, and above all else, loyal. Desdemona's attitudes also represent the worst consequences for women embracing without question the values of a patriarchal society. She would rather die at her husband's hand than live in his distrust. Many modern readers find her position difficult to justify, others find it frankly repugnant. Kate, Shake-speare's heroine from *The Taming of the Shrew,* seems to stand in utter opposition to Desdemona, at least for the better part of the play. Kate is vocal, independent, lonely, and suspicious. Kate seems unwilling to make the compromises necessary for marriage while Desdemona makes so many compromises she is destroyed by her marriage. In *The Unlikely Romance of Kate Bjorkman* Plummer's heroine struggles to find an identity, which avoids the pitfalls that entrap Kate and the webs that ensnare Desdemona.

High school student Kate Bjorkman's usually happy Christmas hol-idays are interrupted when her older brother makes a surprise visit with his new wife and two college friends in tow. With witty insights and a generous dash of self-deprecating humor, Kate retells the events attempting to simultaneously be truthful and write a romance novel. Conflicts arise in all corners—her characters refuse to behave accord-ing to type. Her antagonist and rival, Fleur, turns out to be a wonder-ful friend. And her best friend, Ashley, turns out to be a jealous and dangerous adversary. Richard, her hero, certainly makes Kate's heart flutter, but not enough to warrant a three-paragraph long kiss, the way *The Romance Writer's Handbook* instructs. Kate's attempts to star in and narrate her own happily-ever-after romance are both amusing and heartwarming.

Threaded lightly through the story is a cautionary examination of the misguided "romantic" behavior of Shakespearean heroines, espe-cially Desdemona. Struggling with a topic for her research paper for an advanced Shakespeare class, Kate toys with the idea of writing about Desdemona's innocence. But Fleur, one of the holiday guests in her home, introduces her to feminist criticism as they debate the topic:

> "Her innocence has nothing to do with anything," she said. Her arms were folded loosely on her chest, teacher style. "I mean," she continued, "what if she *hadn't* been innocent? What if she'd slept with Cassio and Brabantio and the entire Italian navy?"
> "Yeah?" My mouth probably hung open. I wasn't sure where she was heading.
> "Would it be okay for him to kill her if she'd been sleeping around? What if he'd been right about her?"
> "But he wasn't right—"
> "But what if he were? What if she were guilty? Is it okay for a hus-band to kill his wife for adultery?"
> "I've never thought about it," I said. "But, no, it wouldn't be right, and yet we're all reading the play as if it's perfectly all right to—" (28)

Fleur forces Kate to reexamine her position from a different point of view, just as Emilia does for Desdemona in *Othello*. Fleur's simple explication of the assumptions implicit in one of the great tragic ro-mances of the Western canon challenges Kate to rethink some of her own assumptions about love and female behavior. Fleur reinforces the point several days later as she and Kate search for articles at the local university library: "Desdemona reminds me of my mother. My mother sees her future husband's 'visage' in her mind. She consecrates herself to them. All of them. And in the end all of her husbands strangle her—metaphorically speaking, of course" (139–40). Both young women recognize the transformational power of romantic illusions and how quickly they can convert a heroine into a victim.

By the time Kate's hero betrays her, Kate has developed the self-confidence to reject romantic victimhood. When she finds Richard succumbing to the temptations of the very voluptuous Ashley at the family New Year's Eve party, Kate tells him off and leaves. Her experience gives her a new insight into Shakespeare's play: "But when I thought of Richard, I felt only a hot anger. I began to feel more sympathy for Trish, and for Othello too. I didn't want to make up. I wanted Richard dead" (165).

But in the end Kate softens without wilting. She recognizes Richard's offer to sleep outside in a snow cave until she forgives him as both suicidal and melodramatic. She accepts his apology and comes to the realization that building a relationship is harder than having a romance. Furthermore, Kate decides to apply to Columbia University, choosing a college for herself rather than applying to the local university Richard will be attending as a graduate student.

In *The Unlikely Romance of Kate Bjorkman*, Plummer creates a light-hearted criticism of the role of women in Shakespeare's *Othello* and offers instead a healthier vision of romantic realism. In addition, she introduces her readers to real feminism through Fleur's support and help. No longer will Kate accept the subtle manipulations and competition for masculine attention offered by Ashley as a substitution for meaningful female friendship. Kate learns to take pride in her individuality and strengths—her unglamorous glasses, her love of linguistics, her charmingly idiosyncratic family—instead of relying on cardboard stereotypes and cloying cliches. As Kate admits herself in the early pages of the book, she shares a name with the protagonist from *The Taming of the Shrew*, the most spirited of Shakespeare's heroines, and it is clearly a fortuitous parallel.

Shakespeare and Anti-Semitism

Whether *Othello* or *The Merchant of Venice* contains the most troublesome material for modern Shakespearean audiences seems a moot point. Both plays are especially difficult because they revel in social and cultural conflicts still unresolved four hundred years after their creation. Yet, both plays appeal for the same reasons. They offer enticing food for thought—not only about where we are, but also about how we got here.

Not surprisingly, my research for this book turned up no young adult novels revising or adapting Shakespeare's *The Merchant of Venice*. Given the vicious results of anti-Semitism in the twentieth century, it is difficult to envision this play as an inviting medium for experimentation. Nonetheless, *The Merchant of Venice* cannot be ignored. It is in many ways the most distinguished piece of anti-Semitism in the Western canon. Were it authored by virtually anyone other than Shakespeare, it probably would have faded from view years ago.

Every production of *The Merchant of Venice* creates tension. Many students of the play believe the story is too ugly to preserve as living drama. Shylock suffers a variety of spiteful degradations in the play. Other people believe that Shakespeare shows thoughtful sympathy and insight into Shylock's plight enabling him to rise far above the entrenched anti-Semitism of Renaissance England, even if he never entirely escapes the biases of his culture. Some people enjoy debating these points; others grow quickly incensed that anyone would label Shakespeare an anti-Semite or, conversely, that anyone would fail to see his anti-Semitism. *The Merchant of Venice* is treacherous ground—reading or producing the play is very likely to produce contention. The basic question boils down to whether the play will help audiences understand the history of anti-Semitism (including modern outgrowths like the Holocaust) and end such prejudices or whether producing the play will only serve to reinforce and continue these prejudices. There is no easy answer to this question, though it is certainly worthy of discussion.

Controversy, in and of itself, is not, however, a reason to avoid the play, but it is reason to engage in some preparation. Much of the tension surrounding *The Merchant of Venice* is due to the fact that audiences are ill-informed about the prejudices of the period. The world of the Renaissance was different from our own. We struggle against prejudice in many ways—with more success in some venues and communities than in others. The people of the Renaissance generally embraced prejudice; non-Christians were regularly and legally discriminated against. To understand the play, audiences need to understand the practices of the community in which it was originally written and performed.

Many European countries outlawed Judaism during the Renaissance. For example, Spain commanded all Jews within its boundaries to convert or leave in 1492. England expelled all Jews even earlier in 1290 and did not make any formal overtures to allow Jews back into the country until 1656. Of course, not every Jewish family left when a country announced expulsion measures. Very small Jewish populations continued to exist in these countries, but they were generally forced to practice their religion only secretly and lived precarious lives. All kinds of terrible lies were circulated about Jews in this period. For example, they were rumored to kill children and poison wells, among other malicious crimes (Shapiro 1996, 91, 97). Unfortunately, many people believed these lies and treated every Jew, should they happen to meet any, as dangerous and vicious criminals. These attitudes are apparent in Shakespeare's play where Shylock is regularly called names and even spat upon.

In countries where Jews were not expelled, like Italy, they were subjected to particularly harsh laws. Most professional jobs in the Renaissance were tied to the church—all formal political, legal, and medical education came through church-controlled universities. Since Jews didn't belong to the Christian church, they weren't allowed to hold most jobs. On the other hand, at least one kind of work was forbidden to Christians—money lending.

Renaissance Christians believed that it was acceptable to loan money to friends or business associates, but it was ungodly to collect interest on such loans. Yet, as trade expanded and time progressed, Christians were allowed to charge some interest on loans but not as high an interest rate as many desired. For example, in 1571 England created a statute that permitted individuals to charge up to ten percent interest on loans (Shapiro 98). Charging interest was called "usury." These moral suspicions about charging interest and legal limitations to the practice were based on the religious belief that God wanted only living things to increase. For example, if a farmer put two sheep together in a pasture, they might naturally reproduce, even have twins, and the next year the farmer would have four sheep. Or he might have three or two or even none—depending on weather, disease, and other conditions outside the farmer's control. But, in any case, the outcome would be dependent on God's will and the farmer should trust in it. If, however, the farmer buried two gold coins in his field, it was perfectly obvious that the number would not increase. No matter how many seasons passed, the two coins would not reproduce themselves. In the Renaissance this was considered evidence that God didn't want money to expand on its own—that charging interest was against God's will. Shylock and Antonio debate this issue using the Biblical story of the shepherds Jacob and Laban in Act 1, scene 3 of the play.

But since charging interest is a very useful economic tool, the people of the Renaissance weren't happy placing such restrictive limitations on loans and interest rates. Instead, they decided that it would be acceptable for Jews to loan money and charge higher rates of interest. According to Christian belief in this period, Jews were damned already, so breaking one more of God's laws was not a particular concern. These Renaissance Christians figured that allowing Jews to be the usurers for the society would enable Christian businesses to grow while ensuring that all the sin would be the fault of the Jews. Obviously, it was a very manipulative and selfish way to do business. Some Christians even went so far as to say that it was a Christian duty to take loans from Jews because this would ensure their condemnation—some of these Christians believed that enticing other people into sin proved their own godliness. Such beliefs are hard for us to understand these days—both Christianity and Judaism have changed a great deal since then.

But in the Renaissance, some Jews were usurers because it was one of the few professions they were legally allowed to practice. Nonetheless, some Christians, like the merchant Antonio in the play, attacked Jews for participating in the very work they were legally thrust into accepting.

Another problem for Jews in Italy during the Renaissance was that they weren't considered full citizens. It did not matter how many years they or their ancestors had lived in Italy, because one of the requirements for being a citizen was being a Christian. In the Renaissance, cities and countries sometimes had several different sets of laws—a more lenient set for citizens and a stricter set for "aliens" or noncitizens. This double legal standard meant that Jews could be punished for things that weren't considered crimes for Christians. An example of this happens late in the play when Shylock is accused of having threatened Antonio's life. The sentence for this crime (an alien threatening a citizen) was execution. But if Antonio threatened Shylock's life, nothing would happen to him. Even though *The Merchant of Venice* is a play concerned with issues of justice, to the modern audience it is clear that the laws of that period were not very fair. As James Shapiro remarks in his book *Shakespeare and the Jews* (1996), this is one of the most troubling scenes of the play. It allows the Venetians to have their cake and eat it too. Venice thrives as a center of international trade specifically because the city's charter guarantees everyone equal legal treatment, yet at the same time Venice appears to have laws that supersede this charter (Shapiro 188). Shapiro carefully explicates the slippery accusations that enable Shakespeare to create a fictional world where Shylock can be simultaneously a resident Jew and an alien moneylender. Whether or not the real Venetian courts would have propagated such a set of contradictory judgments is less important than the fact that to Shakespeare's audiences they would not have appeared unreasonable or incredible.

Perhaps one of the values of studying this play is that it gives audiences a greater appreciation for our own national principle of separating church and state. Since Congress is forbidden from making any religion into the national religion, people of many different religions can use the legal system without fear of religious discrimination. Some people feel the difficult issues involving religious discrimination make the play particularly inappropriate for younger audiences, yet others might hold that these complicated issues are exactly what make it important.

Shylocks and Antonios: Examining Editions of the Play

Mary and Charles Lambs' version of *The Merchant of Venice* within their collection called *Tales from Shakespeare* (1807) represents the very best reasons many teachers shy away from presenting the play to young readers. The Lambs' edition forefronts the anti-Semitism of the play by preserving the ugliest elements of Shylock's character and expunging all the sympathetic elements with which Shakespeare imbued him. The Lambs announce their anti-Semitic agenda with their opening paragraph:

> Shylock, the Jew, lived at Venice: he was an usurer, who had amassed an immense fortune by lending money at great interest to Christian merchants. Shylock, being a hard-hearted man, exacted the payment of the money he lent with such severity that he was much disliked by all good men, and particularly by Antonio, a young merchant of Venice; and Shylock as much hated Antonio, because he used to lend money to people in distress, and would never take any interest for the money he lent; therefore there was a great enmity between this covetous Jew and the generous merchant Antonio. (85)

This version of the play protects readers from having to do any careful thinking about the drama's primary conflict. The Lambs label Shylock as the unmitigated villain and Antonio as the unquestioned hero. These caricatures of Shakespeare's characters are reinforced throughout the tale with smaller labels. Antonio is referred to as "the kindest man that ever lived" while Shylock is spoken of as "the merciless Jew," "cruel Shylock," and "this currish Jew." Although a paraphrase of Portia's famous speech about the quality of mercy is included in the tale, Shylock's equally powerful and poignant speech regarding the feelings of Jews is left out.

Arthur Rackham's famous illustrations (originally added to the text in 1899 and revised in 1909) only add visual ammunition to the Lambs' stereotypical portrait of Shylock. Rackham's Shylock (the only illustration to accompany this tale) stands sharpening his knife against the sole of his shoe. Rackham composed the picture beautifully; a reader's eye is drawn along a diagonal that begins at the top of the frame in Shylock's squinting eyes and elongated face, down the curving collar of his robe (which mirrors the shape of his knife), toward his wrist, which extends to hold a long blade. This illustration of Shylock is as unambiguous in its villainy as the Lambs' description of him.

It is difficult to imagine a circumstance in which this tale could usefully be presented in isolation to modern readers. The Lambs' edition does not do justice to the complexity of Shakespeare's original and instead seems intent on propagating anti-Semitism. Yet, for mature readers already familiar with Shakespeare's original, this tale can provide a useful case study in the shapes of western anti-Semitism and the ways in which a powerful cultural icon like Shakespeare can be manipulated for many purposes—sometimes compelling, but in this case, distressing.

In her 1900 collection of Shakespeare tales, Edith Nesbit takes a wildly different approach to introducing *The Merchant of Venice* to young readers. Although Nesbit admits in her preface that she was influenced and inspired by the Lambs' edition for children, this tale shows her edition is not without originality. The term "Jew" appears nowhere in Nesbit's tale. Nesbit describes Shylock simply as a "rich money-lender" while Antonio is a "rich, smug merchant" (21). Nesbit, like Lamb, also must eliminate Shylock's impassioned plea for compassion since it is built on a rhetorical comparison between Jews and all others and would not make sense in a tale in which the religious and cultural connotations carried by labels like "Jews" and "Christians" have been removed.

Nesbit's version raises many questions. Why has the term "Jew" been eliminated? Is Nesbit trying to preserve Shakespeare from appearing anti-Semitic? Does she want to emphasize the relationship between justice and mercy without becoming entangled in religious and cultural conflicts? Is the term "money-lender" simply an encoded label for "Jew"?

Unlike the Lambs' edition, Nesbit's might serve as a thought-provoking introduction to Shakespeare's text. Reading this short version first might help students recognize how many cultural stereotypes they bring with them to the play. Do readers of Nesbit's tale automatically discuss Shylock as a Jew even though she never mentions this aspect of his character? How do readers understand the conflict and hostility between Antonio and Shylock without the convenient labels "Christian" and "Jew"? At the end of Nesbit's tale Shylock receives a harsh judicial sentence because he is a "foreigner" (28). How do novice readers of the tale make sense of this scene? Is the tale reduced to a simple parable about greed—greedy men invite dislike and eventually are punished by losing their children and their fortune? Or, has Nesbit opened up a refreshing angle on *The Merchant of Venice?*

Leon Garfield's version of the tale in *Shakespeare Stories* (1985) creates a very different portrait of Shylock. Garfield presents the most complete edition of Shakespeare's play. The scenes at Belmont, the casket lottery, and Jessica's elopement with Lorenzo play very little part in the Lambs' and Nesbit's editions. Garfield includes these subplots and details them as carefully as he does the conflict between Antonio and Shylock.

Garfield's edition makes good use of narrative form. He pays close attention to atmosphere and uses it to help shape his characters. His first introduction of Shylock illustrates this technique. Garfield describes Bassanio's search for Shylock:

> In a narrow street, where the water ran dark and crooked between high weeping walls, and little barred windows, like imprisoned eyes, stared dully down, he had met with a lean, bearded man in black, who smiled and frowned and smiled and frowned, and rubbed his hands together as if he would get to the bone of them. Shylock was his name, and he was a Jew.
>
> He was not a man to Bassanio's liking, nor to the liking of any Venetian, for he seemed to crawl across the fair fabric of the city like a spider, spoiling it. But he lent money. (79)

The images of confinement and entrapment—from the walls to the windows to the web the spider-like Shylock spins create an eerie and disconcerting atmosphere. Garfield goes on, however, to explain to readers that Shylock's circumstances are not of his own making:

> Money was the Jew's only commodity, and the Christian undermined him. The Christian could make money out of trade; the Jew, by Venetian law, could only make money out of money. Take away his money and you take away his life. For these reasons the dark Jew hated the bright Christians of Venice; and, strongest of all, he hated them because they hated him. Hate breeds hate as fast as summer flies. (80)

With only a few lines of context, Garfield enlightens readers to the legal constraints, which stand as the foundation for Antonio and Shylock's conflict and mutual hostility.

Michael Foreman's illustration of Shylock standing in court testing the tip of his knife against his index finger makes a wonderful comparison with Rackham's illustration in the Lambs' text. All of the compassion Garfield's edition generates for Shylock shines through Foreman's picture (facing page 96). Just as in the Rackham illustration, Shylock dominates the picture, but this Shylock looks both forlorn and anxious. He shows no anticipation about collecting his bond from Antonio. Conversely, the eyes of the citizens gathered in the courtroom glimmer in the background of the illustration threateningly. Shylock is not the predator here; he is the prey hunted and cornered by the laws of Venice.

Even in Garfield's careful edition, however, Shylock is still in some ways represented as the villain. He "scuttles," he "screams," he "raves," and he "glares." Antonio, Bassanio, and Portia seem much better-balanced characters. In the end, Garfield also seems to approve of

Shylock's forced conversion to Christianity under threat of death. In Shakespeare's play Shylock agrees to the conditions of his pardon with only the barest acknowledgement, "I am content" (4.2.394). In Garfield's edition of the play, Shylock leaves the court head bowed,

> to embrace a gentler God than the one that had brought him. As he went, the thronged candles tugged after him, as if to lend him a little of the radiance of a court in which, not justice, not the law, but mercy had triumphed. (98)

Garfield seems to imply that Shylock accepts the conditions of the court and is even on his way to being grateful for a decision that strips him of his identity and his livelihood (as a Christian he can no longer act as a money lender). Shakespeare's play leaves a great deal more room for interpretation. Garfield's tale is tidier than Shakespeare's. Audiences of the drama often wonder what becomes of Shylock after he disappears at the end of Act Four; Garfield solves this problem making the conclusion of his tale a much more unified "happy ending."

Conclusions

Othello and *The Merchant of Venice* provide wonderful opportunities for making Shakespeare meaningful to modern audiences. Although we may decry our own inability to rid ourselves of stereotypes and prejudices rooted in race, religion, and culture, Shakespeare provides readers with a thought-provoking lens for exploring how deeply these problems are embedded in Western civilization and how far we've come in eradicating them. Reading *Othello* and *The Merchant of Venice* may help young adults take a longer view in discussions and debates about the value of affirmative action and the separation of church and state—these are modern problems, and at the same time they are ancient ones. The wealth of modern editions and revisions of these plays provide terrific windows for looking both outward at the larger world and inward at ourselves.

Chapter Nine

A Tragedy in the Classroom: The Disappearance of Comedies and Histories

When Stephen Sondheim wrote the lyrics for the Broadway musical *A Funny Thing Happened on the Way to the Forum* (1962), which, coincidentally, shares the same source as Shakespeare's *A Comedy of Errors*, the Roman comedian Plautus, he titled his opening number "Comedy Tonight." The American education system seems to have adopted an entirely different motto: "Tragedy Tonight and Tomorrow and Tomorrow and Tomorrow." Yet, the tragedies make up merely twenty-five percent of Shakespeare's plays. The comedies and histories make up the rest of his work.

Both of these genres have characteristics that might make them seem difficult or unapproachable. The comedies are burdened by a generic title frequently misleading to modern readers. Most of *The Merchant of Venice*, a Shakespearean comedy, seems distinctly unamusing to today's audiences—which is part of the reason I paired my discussion of that play in the previous chapter with a clearly tragic play, *Othello*. Obviously, the Renaissance definitions of genre vary greatly from our own. We tend to associate the "comic" solely with laughter—many people think of the physical comedy, lewd jokes, and exaggerated parodies typical on television sit-coms. When literary scholars or printers of the sixteenth and seventeenth centuries used the term *comedy*, they were referring to dramas that affirmed the continuity of the family and society. In this sense, any play that ends either with marriages or with promises of marriage is termed a comedy. Most of these plays also contain moments of verbal punning (especially sexual innuendoes), a selection of sly or witty characters, generous opportunities for physical clowning, and other varieties of humor, but they must always feature marriage. The prospects for these unions do not necessarily even have to look particularly happy. In *Two Gentlemen of Verona* Julia is given in marriage to Proteus, who has already shown himself to be both a traitor and a would-be rapist. In *Measure for Measure* Isabelle receives a proposal she almost certainly can't refuse from Duke Vincentio; her own goals to become a nun and live in chaste servitude of God must be discarded. In *Twelfth Night* a disguise and a case of mistaken identity lead Olivia to marry a complete stranger; she only discovers her error after the ceremony. Very few of us would find such situations truly comic; they seem more like recipes for disaster and marital discord. Yet, all these plays are labeled Shakespearean comedies.

During the Renaissance most theater goers probably didn't worry about such categories at all. Although scholars speculate that playbills posted outside the theaters and perhaps around London might have announced the name of the day's performance, there is a good chance many customers did not know what play they would see until they arrived at the theater (Gurr 1992, 11). Instead of choosing a particular play, many people probably trusted in the reputation each theater developed. Over the course of time most theaters developed a specialty. Just as many modern movie goers today know that certain theaters specialize in featuring the absolute newest release while others, usually smaller theaters in larger cities, feature art house favorites or foreign films, Renaissance play goers knew that one playhouse tended to produce action-packed dramas with lots of military conflicts, while another theater, perhaps a bit more run down, tended to perform only old favorites (Gurr 229–30). These citizens didn't concern themselves with labels like "comedy" or "tragedy" and modern readers should be wary of relying too heavily on them as well.

In part to deal with the schism between what modern readers expect in a comedy and what they are liable to find in a play, many literary critics have further divided Shakespeare's comedies into subcategories. Plays like *The Merchant of Venice, All's Well That Ends Well,* and *Measure for Measure,* which contain particularly disturbing elements, are frequently discussed as "problem plays." Plays like *The Tempest, A Winter's Tale,* and *Pericles,* which involve multigenerational conflicts, a high number of coincidences, and magical elements, are labeled "romances." The best known of Shakespeare's comedies are those that revel in the silliness and excitement of new-found love. These plays usually put lovers to some sort of test, but ultimately demonstrate an optimistic attitude toward human relationships. Plays like *As You Like It* or *Much Ado*

About Nothing fall into this category, but the best known of them all is certainly *A Midsummer Night's Dream.*

The Comedy of Love: *A Midsummer Night's Dream*

Two young adult authors present revisions of this popular drama within their novels. The first of these, Marilyn Singer's *The Course of True Love Never Did Run True* (1983), takes its name from a line in the play. With its four sets of lovers all fighting or exchanging partners, *A Midsummer Night's Dream* shares a great deal with the typical high school social scene. Singer takes full advantage of this opportunity by setting her story in New York City's Euclid High School during a production of Shakespeare's comedy. Tensions begin to grow when auditions are opened up to include seniors, instead of just juniors. Neither lovers nor actors appreciate unexpected competition. Of course, not everyone gets the role he or she desires, but the novel's narrator, Becky, does win the coveted opportunity to play Hermia.

Throughout the production the students struggle both to understand the meaning of love and to understand the meaning of the play. Parental love confuses Marisa; her suspicious and overbearing father won't let her date and insists on viewing all women as potential tramps. Romantic love confuses Craig and Richie, who are struggling to express and find acceptance of their homosexuality. Platonic love plagues Nemi and Becky, who have enjoyed a deep friendship for years but yearn for something more glamorous and exciting. These confusions are reflections of Shakespeare's complex treatment of love in *A Midsummer Night's Dream.* In the play, Egeus threatens his daughter Hermia with death when she refuses his choice of groom—an exceptional example of parental love gone astray. Quarrelsome Titania and Oberon demonstrate the challenges of marital love. And, most famously, the confused and inconstant quartet of lovers who wander off into the woods—Hermia, Helena, Demetrius, and Lysander—illuminate the problems that arise when friendship runs afoul of romantic love. By the end of the novel, like the play, everyone has found a partner, and all of the students have achieved a more complex understanding of the multifaceted experience of love.

The discussions of the meaning of *A Midsummer Night's Dream* may be even more helpful for young adult readers. Singer infuses characters with a vision or interpretation of the play that reflects his or her own struggles. Leila claims:

> It is a play about the meaning of love and about the illusions we all have. It's a play about growth through trial. After all, a dream is a trip into the unconscious. Confusing, irrational, frightening even. But if

we allow ourselves to look at our dreams—to experience them—we can learn a lot. (68)

As the most attractive and sophisticated of the students, Leila is herself an illusion for at least one of her fellow actors, who has difficulty distinguishing between her appearance and her character. But Leila is herself driven by dreams—she wants to become a professional actress.

Becky interprets the play very differently:

> I wonder if even Theseus and Hippolyta learn something through what they hear about what the others experienced. . . . Like how their marriage can't work if it's based on jealousy or anger or just lust . . . I mean infatuation. . . . Hermia and Lysander and Demetrius and Helena have to learn that love is not infatuation. And Hippolyta and Theseus have to have real love, too, to make a good marriage. (69)

Becky's observations about the play foreshadow the recognition she will need to reach regarding her own relationship with Nemi before the novel ends. Exploring the relationships among Shakespeare's characters helps prepare her to explore her own ideas about love and friendship. At the end of the novel while down with the flu, Becky reads an essay about the play, which enables her to make some connections between Shakespeare's world and her own:

> Most of the stuff I read talked about dating the play or the characters of Bottom or Theseus or the nature of comedy. But one essay struck me as interesting. It talked about the main theme of the play—the transitoriness, inconstancy and irrationality of love—and that got me thinking about everything I'd been going through concerning love, about what that four-letter word really means. I went mad over Blake, and then, poof, nothing, or, at least, next to nothing. Nice play, Shakespeare. Love sure is transitory, irrational, inconstant, all right. (208)

Unlike many young adult novels that reinterpret Shakespeare, Singer's book makes such regular and complex reference to the characters and events of the play that readers without any previous introduction to *A Midsummer Night's Dream* might find some episodes difficult to understand. Surely, this technique limits the audience for Singer's book, but for those readers who have spent some time with the play, the novel offers a great opportunity to explore different interpretations of the drama. In this way Singer provides her readers with the opportunity to read a type of critical theory and enjoy a witty plot all at the same time.

Terry Pratchett approaches *A Midsummer Night's Dream* very differently in *Lords and Ladies* (1992), a novel in his Discworld series of fantasy tales. Although the Discworld novels have frequent connections from one volume to the next, each reads independently. Pratchett's novels often begin with figures borrowed from myth and literature—no one from Santa Claus to Shakespeare is safe—and puts them into play on a planet teeming with magic, witty dialogue, wild adventures, and every other variation of humor and unpredictability his imagination can muster.

Lords and Ladies takes up more or less where Pratchett's *Wryd Sisters* (1988) left off. *Wyrd Sisters* is itself a reinterpretation of *Macbeth* and receives its own discussion in Chapter 5. In *Lords and Ladies,* Magrat, the youngest and most romantic witch in the small country of Lancre, is making ready to marry the recently crowned King Verence. Several local craftsmen agree to put on a play to help celebrate the wedding, but the play they select happens to be about a group of rustic tradesmen putting on a play. One parody of Shakespeare nests within another in Pratchett's typical style. Like Shakespeare's "rude mechanicals" in *A Midsummer Night's Dream,* these craftsmen also have a great deal of trouble understanding the traditions of drama. To start off with, they aren't even sure what "rude mechanicals" or "artisans" are, and the Latinate stage directions, like *Exeunt Omnes,* confuse them further (106). Many readers, as unfamiliar with Renaissance terminology as Pratchett's characters, are likely to sympathize with them.

The more closely Pratchett's craftsmen study the play, however, the less they like it. In fact, they find it downright insulting and see it as evidence of the snobbish urban attitudes of playwrights toward hardworking country folk. What's more, rehearsals are not going well:

> "Don't work, does it?" said Thatcher.
> "S'not funny, that I do know," said Weaver. "Can't see the king killing himself laughing at us playing a bunch of mechanical artisans not being very good at doin' a play."
> "You're just no good at it," said Jason.
> "We're *sposed* to be no good at it," said Weaver.
> "Yeah, but you're no good at acting like someone who's no good at acting," said Tinker. (179)

They also find the idea of a play with a donkey in it almost too funny to bear. All in all, they can't help wishing for the old days when the only thing needed to celebrate a wedding was a traditional dance or two.

Pratchett parodies the romantic elements of Shakespeare's play as well. The novel is filled with unlikely and unexpected romances, but instead of happening amongst the courtiers, as they do in *A Midsummer Night's Dream,* they happen amongst the witches in the country. Ancient Granny Weatherwax finds herself reunited with a lover from long ago, Wizard Ricully. Lusty Nanny Ogg finds herself entangled with a dwarf named Casanunda (as his name implies, he isn't quite Cassanova, but that doesn't stop him from trying). Magrat, of course, finds her romance in her marriage to the practical but somewhat obtuse King Verence. Other lesser characters also find themselves baited and tempted by love.

Shakespeare's play wouldn't be complete without the fairies whose initial dispute seems in some ways to explain the existence of so much disquiet in the realms of human love. Pratchett arranges for a similar source of conflict in his novel, but he blames the fairies much more overtly than does Shakespeare. In *A Midsummer Night's Dream* Oberon, Titania, and even Puck, ultimately prove helpful to the human lovers. In *Lords and Ladies* fairies are a threat. Only the vigilance and hard work of the three witches, Granny Weatherwax, Nanny Ogg, and Magrat, keeps them from breaking out of their own world and overrunning everyone else's.

Unlike Singer's novel, *Lords and Ladies* plays with Shakespeare's drama without any particular system and without reaching toward any particular interpretation. Instead, Pratchett seems merely to juggle with the themes, characters, and ideas introduced by Shakespeare. At some points in the novel this juggling enables new points of view, but at other points it produces primarily the humor that comes from looking at the familiar from unfamiliar or incongruous angles. Pratchett tosses more than just *A Midsummer Night's Dream* about in this book, however. Perdita, a character from *A Winter's Tale,* makes a sort of appearance, and a young hero named Shawn unwittingly imitates the St. Crispin's Day speech from *Henry V* (328). Lovers of English witchcraft lore may also marvel at the ways Pratchett has woven names like "Agnes" and "Device" into the text—references to a set of infamous witches from Lancaster County prosecuted in 1612. Most readers will not, however, notice these clever allusions. Instead, they will lose themselves in the fast-paced, witty, and ribald dialogue that marks Pratchett's writing.

The Mystery of History: *Richard III*

Shakespeare's history plays are often a hard sell. In their day, they featured names and events familiar to the audiences. Only the least educated among the crowd would wonder which Lord might win the crown or whether the attractive princess would succumb to the hero's romantic banter as they watched young Hal battle Hotspur in *The First Part of Henry IV* or King Henry woo Katherine in *Henry V.* Instead, the crowds found enjoyment watching well-known national glories unfold, viewing great military victories re-created, and seeing the figures of myth fleshed out with faults and virtues on full display. Modern audiences, especially in the United States, have a great deal more trouble understanding the history plays these days. Often readers come to the plays with no knowledge of the characters, places, and events so important to understanding and appreciating the story. Few teachers or students have the time to immerse themselves in the study of British history necessary to make sense of it all. Even with a thorough background in this material, not all audiences will appreciate the history plays, which often feature character development over plot twists, as much as they will other forms of drama.

Despite these significant handicaps, some of Shakespeare's history plays still hold a great deal of theatrical power. *The First Part of Henry IV* teems with enticing characters. Falstaff's criminal mischief and self-serving escapades, Hotspur's vivid rhetoric and swift actions, and Hal's family friction and personal redemption appeal to many audiences. Other plays feature figures likely to intrigue young adults. *The First Part of Henry VI*, not one of Shakespeare's best-appreciated works, includes Joan De Pucelle—better known as Joan of Arc. The story of the teen-age war leader, mystic, and martyr has recently been retold by Barbara Dana in *Young Joan* (1991) and Nancy Garden in *Dove and Sword* (1995). In *Recasting the Past: The Middle Ages in Young Adult Literature* (2000), Rebecca Barnhouse explains the artful and artless ways Joan's history has been revised and refashioned to make her appealing in the modern era. Exploring the treatment of Joan in literature and drama, from the French perspective and from the English point of view, gives readers a new way to appreciate how art and history intertwine.

Richard III also retains popularity. The rise and fall of a charismatic villain reverberates with contemporary parallels in virtually any time and place. *Richard III* benefits too from the glamour of an unsolved mystery. Just as Richard's rule began, his two young nephews—both of whom boasted a claim to the throne stronger than Richard's own—disappeared without a trace. Were they murdered by Richard or one of his henchmen? Did they die suddenly of disease or from a legitimate accident? Were they spirited off to another country for safekeeping? No one knows, but most people suspect the worst.

This mystery has made explorations of the historical figure of Richard III more readily available than, perhaps, any other major figure in Shakespeare's historical dramas. Thoughtful research into his policies and government has led many historians, amateur and professional, toward unbridled enthusiasm for this much-maligned King. The Richard the Third Society, established in 1924, produces a scholarly journal and a Web site aimed at rescuing this English ruler from undeserved infamy and scorn. In 1951 the well-known mystery writer Josephine Tey produced a novel exploring Richard's supposed crimes entitled *The Daughter of Time;* this is just one of the nearly three hundred novels set in the fifteenth century featuring Richardian themes listed in the library catalog of The Richard the Third Society. Obviously, there is plenty of meat here for young adult readers interested in exploring England's most famous royal villain. One of the more recent offerings in this vein, John Ford's *The Dragon Waiting: A Masque of History* (1983), posits an alternative history in which Richard is not only redeemed from any criminal slurs but survives to lead England as its undisputed and much-appreciated ruler.

Much of the appeal of each of these novels is due to genre conventions. Tey's traditional mystery style will appeal to some, but given the recent vogue for vampire fiction, many young adult readers with an interest in history and a taste for the fantastic may prefer the gothic imagination of Ford. Ford's complex novel begins by introducing, one by one, the four characters whose fates eventually weave together and provide the impetus for the plot. Hywel Peredur ap Owain, a young Welsh boy, follows the unspoken voice of a wizard and finds his vocation in the sorcerer's art. Dimitrios Ducas begins life as the son of a provincial governor on the outskirts of the Roman Empire. Political betrayal sends him out to make his own fortune as a soldier and military leader at a young age. Cynthia Ricci comes from a family of skilled and influential Italian doctors. But the ability to dispense medicines is not very different from the ability to administer poisons, and Cynthia soon finds herself entangled in deadly intrigues and blackmailing schemes. The vampire Gregory von Bayern holds a special appeal for many modern readers. In Ford's world, vampires are real; most are despised and hunted for the toll they take on human lives, but those with the self-discipline to feed off animal blood instead of human blood can earn respect and power.

All four of these characters become involved in the political intrigues of the Byzantine Empire, France, and England. Eventually, they take service with Richard Plantagenet (Richard III). Readers familiar with Shakespeare's play will discover a very different set of family relationships among the British royals than those imagined in the famous play. Instead of being the treacherous brother, Richard is depicted as the only reliable man in a corrupt family. In Shakespeare's play, Richard's mother despises him:

> O my accursed womb, the bed of death!
> A cockatrice hast thou hatch'd to the world,
> Whose unavoided eye is murtherous. (4.1.53–55)

In Ford's novel, conversely, Richard's mother compares him with his siblings to declare he is her favored child: "I have a brave son, who became a gluttonous king, and a pretty son, who has become a treacherous fool. Richard is angry, but is the most constant of my boys still living" (183). Similarly, Richard is implicated in the death of his wife Queen Anne in the play but is devoted to his "Annie" in the novel.

Ford also posits an unexpected explanation for the secretive disappearance of Richard's two young nephews. Instead of murdering them, one of Richard's rivals has infected them with vampirism. Gifted with eternal life and an unquenchable taste for the blood of their subjects, they present a special kind of threat to the kingdom. Employing the elaborate rituals necessary to dispose of a vampire permanently becomes not a self-indulgent act but a painfully necessary one for anyone interested in protecting the kingdom.

Ford's vision of Richard III obviously depends more on his creative imagination than historical research. As the author himself explains, his purpose is to entertain. Yet, readers familiar with Shakespeare's play and with British history will recognize the factual framework Ford has skillfully redecorated with new possibilities, new characters, and new psychological motivations.

Stephanie Tolan presents a much more traditional approach to exploring *Richard III* in *The Face in the Mirror* (1998). Raised by his mother and his grandfather, fifteen-year-old Jared Kingsley is surprised to learn his father is a famous actor and even more shocked to learn that family circumstances will force him to spend the summer with this stranger. Phillip Kingsley turns out to be quite friendly, however; he even makes room for Jared in his summer stock production of *Richard III*. Jared and his newly met half-brother, Tad, will play Richard's young, doomed nephews.

Jared arrives at the New World Shakespeare Company in Addison, Michigan, with few expectations. Although he has tried to prepare for his role by watching recent film versions of the play, he doesn't have any theater experience. Introducing Jared to the structures of the theater and the rhythms of rehearsal gives Tolan an opportunity to teach her readers about the world of the stage at the same time as her protagonist learns. Similarly, Tolan lets Jared think and talk about *Richard III* a great deal in order to provide readers with a generous sense of Shakespeare's play. Jared says:

> And it's a great story. Richard, the Duke of Gloucester, wants to be king of England when the old king dies, but there are a bunch of other people in line for the crown before him. So he kills them. Or, like a Mafia godfather, has them killed—including his nephews, the two princes Tad and I were going to play. For a while, it looks like the bad guy's going to win—Richard gets the guys around him to do everything he wants them to do, mostly by promising them big rewards when he's in power, and manages to have himself crowned king. But some of his henchmen get scared off by the murders and turn against him, and when he doesn't live up to the promises he made, he loses some others. Finally, he gets killed in a battle to keep his crown. Sad end for Richard, happy end for everyone else, except all the people he's killed. (25)

Tolan takes one other step to help make envisioning the play more approachable for young audiences; Phillip Kingsley has decided to place his production of *Richard III* in a futuristic setting loosely modeled on the world of *Star Wars*. Medieval England may not be very familiar to some readers, but the world of the Empire, stormtroopers, and light sabers probably will be. Purists may shudder (maybe a lot), but even they must admit that each generation remakes Shakespeare in its own image.

The sibling rivalry recorded by Shakespeare between Richard and his brothers soon begins to be played out between Jared and Tad as well. Tad's experience doing television work enhances his sense of superiority over Jared. Like Richard, Tad resents being upstaged by his older brother—whether at rehearsal or during a family dinner. He wants all the limelight for himself. Jared has inherited his mother's good looks, but Tad, like Richard, lacks any physical glamour (his childish charm has been ravaged, at least temporarily, by the onset of adolescence). Tad's lies, petty intrigues, and emotional manipulation serve as a fine foil for the antics of Shakespeare's famous villain.

Tad's undisguised dislike for Jared makes it difficult for the two boys to play their roles very easily. Jared isn't enough of an actor to perform scenes of brotherly affection with a half-brother he'd really prefer to smack. Instead, Jared decides to use their conflicts on stage—he plays his role without trying to hide his distaste for Tad, creating an interpretation of *Richard III* in which the two princes are as much at odds with each other as everyone else:

> All the rest of the way through the scene, there was that edge of rivalry—two brothers who knew exactly what was what now that their father was gone. The words we said were all about royal manners, but underneath there was the knowledge that I was the one who would be king and—because I was there first—there was nothing he could do about it. (87)

Jared finds the praise for his new vision of the role flattering, but enjoys Tad's jealous scowl even more.

Tolan echoes other aspects of Shakespeare's drama in her novel as well. The supernatural—dreams, premonitions, and especially ghosts—plays a central role in *Richard III*. Ghosts also haunt Tolan's novel. Like Richard himself, Tad has a visceral and almost inexplicable fear of ghosts. Although tales of the ghosts who haunt theaters protecting, approving, and sometimes cursing productions are as much a part of most theaters as the stage and the spotlight, the cast members in Phillip Kingsley's production are not supposed to talk of such things in front of Tad. But not everyone can resist, and the tales told by George, one of the other cast members, soon have Jared intrigued. He likes the thought of a ghost, and he likes the thought of taking some revenge upon Tad even better.

Jared initiates a series of small pranks at Tad's expense and blames them on a ghost, hoping to unnerve his half-brother. His ploy works but, much to Jared's shock, soon more dramatic and dangerous antics begin to be discovered—ones he knows nothing about. Eventually, Jared discovers a long, unused section of the theater where he finds an old steamer trunk filled with playbills and theatrical souvenirs, all advertising performances by an actor named Garrick Marsden during the years 1858 to 1887. A poster from an 1859 production of *Richard III* especially intrigues him, but not as much as the spectral vision of Marsden himself, who soon appears to Jared.

Jared develops a complicated relationship with the ghost. Marsden is a trickster; usually Jared enjoys watching the rest of the cast stumble or tremble at the ghost's whim, but sometimes he seems to go too far. Jared also enjoys hearing stories about past productions, especially *Richard III*, which Marsden assures him is guaranteed to be a success in any age. "People," Marsden explains, "can't get enough of Richard— there is something forever compelling about a man who revels in his own evil" (107).

Only slowly does Jared realize that Marsden is speaking about himself as much as he is Richard. The ghost, he learns, doesn't haunt the theater as a friendly mascot; he is waiting for revenge. Betrayed by his own alcoholism and malice, Marsden lost both a coveted role and his life in the Addison theater nearly a century earlier. Jared's discoveries horrify him, but Marsden only revels in the boy's distress—it proves he still has his touch and performed the role of a friendly ghost to perfection. All Marsden's pawns are in place, all his plots have been set into action; his treachery rivals even Richard's! Now, Marsden only wants a death to complete his drama—Tad's murder. Jared needs all his wits and all his acting skills to prevent a tragedy on opening night.

Tolan infuses her novel with themes of rivalry and revenge that effectively reflect and comment on Shakespeare's play. Fans of *Richard III* will enjoy seeing the play from the point of view of the princes—the roles Jared and Tad play—and readers of Tolan's novel will arrive at the play prepared to appreciate the complexities of the plot and the vagaries of Richard's character. Tolan's novel offers much as a prequel to *Richard III* or as a sequel to it.

Conclusions

Shakespeare's prestigious reputation may be almost as much of a liability as it is an asset. American Shakespearean scholars may experience poignant little moments when someone tells us about seeing "a great play that had language like Shakespeare, but it was really good, really funny." Of course, the production turns out to be a Shakespearean comedy. Far too many people, blighted by the limitations of the typical school curriculum, have no conception that many of Shakespeare's plays are supposed to be funny—they've never been introduced to the earthy, slapstick, and silly elements within Shakespearean drama. They don't know Shakespeare wrote anything but tragedy. His histories, if it is possible, are even more misunderstood. Young adult literature provides a fine bridge to cross the gap between Shakespearean genres. Novels are familiar forms and can provide readers with ways to interpret dramatic conventions with which they aren't yet comfortable. And, ultimately, more people get the chance to explore the other three-quarters of Shakespeare's canon!

Afterword

Every month I receive a glossy catalog of forthcoming books from one or more of the larger publishers of children's and young adult books. Throughout the process of writing this volume, I've had a very mixed response to these mailings. I delight in the discovery that a favorite author is about to produce another treat for me, but virtually every time I opened a catalog over the past year, I also discovered a new Shakespeare inspired text—or two. Should I rejoice at uncovering more material for my project or surrender to the fact that I cannot discuss all of it? Sometimes I was able to order the new books immediately—as was the case with Stephanie Tolan's *The Face in the Mirror* (1998) and Gary Blackwood's *The Shakespeare Stealer* (1998). Other times the books weren't yet available—only tantalizing descriptions of them with estimated publication dates. William Wise has a new book entitled *Nell of Branford Hall* (1999) about the plague of Eyam, which sounds as if it might make a fine companion piece to Jill Paton Walsh's *Parcel of Patterns* (1983) and illustrate the gap between the lives of the wealthy and the lives of ordinary adolescents during the seventeenth century. But I don't know because I haven't yet got a hold of this new text. Paula Boock's *Dare Truth or Promise* (1999) includes a high school production of *Twelfth Night* among its plot twists. Shakespeare's comedies are terribly underrepresented in my book, and I would have loved the opportunity to devote more chapters to this genre. But I can't very well recommend a book I haven't read!

Other offerings were tantalizing but beyond the small scope of this volume. Fiona Buckley writes mystery novels that feature Ursula, a Lady of the Prescence Chamber in the court of Queen Elizabeth. The suspense elements make these books particularly appealing to young adult readers—but the material strays a little too far away from Shakespeare for consideration here. Still, when I read that another volume is being released . . . I wish I could find space to discuss Buckley's work.

With Shakespeare experiencing a modern, cultural renaissance in film, in the opening of the New Globe Theater in London, and in other aspects of popular art, we can probably expect more children's and young adult novels and picture books reinterpreting Shakespeare and his work. Hopefully, this book, even though it cannot serve as an introduction to these still unpublished tales, will serve as an inspiration to seek them out and explore how they add to Shakespeare's legacy and our interpretations of his plays.

Works Cited

Primary Texts

Aliki. 1999. *William Shakespeare and the Globe*. New York: HarperCollins.

Aronson, B. 1996. *Wishbone Classics Romeo and Juliet*. Illus. by Hokanson, Cichetti and K. Yingling. New York: HarperPaperbacks.

Avi. 1987. *Romeo and Juliet Together (and Alive!) at Last*. New York: Avon Books.

Belbin, D. 1998. *Love Lessons*. New York: Scholastic Press.

Beneduce, A.K. 1996. *The Tempest*. Illus. G. Spirin. New York: Philomel Books.

Birch, B. 1993. *Shakespeare Stories*. 3 vols. New York: Wing Books.

Blackwood, G. 1998. *The Shakespeare Stealer*. New York: Dutton's Children's Books.

Boock, P. 1999. *Dare Truth or Promise*. Boston: Houghton Mifflin Co.

Burdett, L. 1995. *A Child's Portrait of Shakespeare*. Windsor, Ontario: Black Moss Press.

———1996. *Macbeth for Kids*. Windsor, Ontario: Black Moss Press.

———1997. *A Midsummer Night's Dream for Kids*. Windsor, Ontario: Firefly Books.

———1998. *Romeo and Juliet for Kids*. Windsor, Ontario: Firefly Books.

———1999. *The Tempest for Kids*. Windsor, Ontario: Firefly Books.

———1994. *Twelfth Night for Kids*. Windsor, Ontario: Black Moss Press.

Chute, M. 1956. *Stories from Shakespeare*. Cleveland: The World Publishing Company.

Cooper, S. 1999. *The King of Shadows*. New York: McElderry Books.

Coville, B. 1997. *Macbeth*. Illus. Gary Kelley. New York: Penguin Books.

———1996. *A Midsummer Night's Dream*. Illus. Dennis Nolan. New York: Penguin Books.

———1999. *Romeo and Juliet*. Illus. Dennis Nolan. New York: Penguin Books.

———1994. *The Tempest*. Illus. Ruth Sanderson. New York: Bantam Doubleday Dell.

Covington, D. 1991. *Lizard*. New York: Bantam Doubleday Dell.

Clarke, M.C. 1850–52. *The Girlhood of Shakespeare's Heroines*. 5 vols. London: W. H. Smith and Son, Simpkin, Marshall and Co.

Dana. B. 1991. *Young Joan*. New York: Harper Trophy.

Dhondy, F. 1993. *Black Swan*. Boston: Houghton Mifflin Company.

Draper, S. M. 1994. *Tears of a Tiger*. New York: Aladdin Paperbacks.

Duncan, L. 1978. *Killing Mr. Griffin*. Boston: Little, Brown and Company.

Early, M. 1998. *Romeo and Juliet*. New York: Harry N. Abrams, Inc.

Ford, J. 1983. *The Dragon Waiting: A Masque of History*. New York: Avon.

Garden, N. 1995. *Dove and Sword: A Novel of Joan of Arc*. New York: Scholastic.

Garfield, L. 1990 & 1994. *Shakespeare Stories*. Illus. Michael Foreman. 2 vols. Boston: Houghton Mifflin Co.

Gilmore, K. 1990. *Enter Three Witches*. New York: Scholastic Inc.

———1993. *Jason and the Bard*. Boston: Houghton Mifflin Co.

Graham, H. 1994. *A Boy and His Bear*. New York: Simon and Schuster.

Katz, W.W. 1993. *Come Like Shadows*. Toronto: Puffin Books.

Kincaid. E. 1997. *Macbeth*. Adapted by J. Escott. New Market, England: Brimax.

———1996. *A Midsummer Night's Dream*. Adapted by J. Escott. New Market, England: Brimax.

———1996. *The Tempest*. Adapted by J. Escott. New Market, England: Brimax.

Lamb, M. and C. Lamb. 1907. (Reprinted 1995). *Tales from Shakespeare*. Illus. Arthur Rackham. New York: Quality Paper Book Club.

Langley, A. 1999. *Shakespeare's Theatre*. Illus. by J. Everett. Oxford: Oxford University Press.

L'Engle, M. 1962. *A Wrinkle in Time*. New York: Farrar, Straus, and Giroux.

Lester, J. 1995. *Othello: A Novel*. New York: Scholastic Inc.

Lewis, A. and T. Wynne-Jones. 1994. *Rosie Backstage*. Illus. B. Slavin. Toronto: Kids Can Press Ltd.

Lively, Penelope. 1974. *The House in Norham Gardens*. New York: Dutton.

———1971. *The Whispering Knights*. London: Mammoth.

McCaffrey, A. 1969. *The Ship Who Sang*. London: Corgi Books.

McCaughrean, G. 1987. *A Little Lower Than the Angels*. New York: Oxford University Press.

Mulherin. J. 1989. *As You Like It*. Illus. by G. Thompson. New York: Peter Bedrick Books.

Nesbit, E. 1900. *The Children's Shakespeare*. Philadelphia: Henry Altemus Company.

———1997. *The Best of Shakespeare: Retellings of 10 Classic Plays*. Introduction by I. Opie and Afterword by P. Hunt. Oxford: Oxford University Press.

Oneal, Z. 1985. *In Summer Light*. New York: Bantam Books.

Paterson, K. 1977. *Bridge to Terabithia*. Illus. Donna Diamond. New York: Harper Trophy.

Plummer, L. 1995. *The Unlikely Romance of Kate Bjorkman.* New York: Bantam Double Day Dell Books.

Pratchett, T. 1992. *Lords and Ladies.* London: Corgi Books.

———1988. *Wyrd Sisters.* London: Corgi Books.

Ross, S. 1994. *Shakespeare and Macbeth: The Story Behind the Play.* Illus. T. Karpinski and V. Ambrus. New York: Penguin.

Singer, M. 1983. *The Course of True Love Never Did Run Smooth.* New York: Harper & Row.

Shakespeare, W. 1974. *The Riverside Shakespeare.* Ed. G. Blakemore Evans. Boston: Houghton.

Smiley, J. 1991. *A Thousand Acres.* New York: Fawcett Columbine.

Sonnenmark, L. 1990. *Something's Rotten in the State of Maryland.* New York: Scholastic.

Stanley, D. and P. Vennema. 1992. *The Bard of Avon: The Story of William Shakespeare.* Illus. by D. Stanley. New York: Morrow Junior Books.

Tey, J. 1951. *The Daughter of Time.* New York: Macmillan Company.

Tolan, S.S. 1998. *The Face in the Mirror.* New York: Morrow Junior Books.

Trease, G. 1940. *Cue for Treason.* London: Puffin Books.

Walsh, J.P. 1983. *A Parcel of Patterns.* New York: Farrar, Straus and Giroux.

Williams, T. 1994. *Caliban's Hour.* New York: Harper Paperbacks.

Wise, W. 1999. *Nell of Branford Hall.* New York: Penguin Putnam Inc.

Secondary Texts

Allen, B. 1991. "A School Perspective on Shakespeare Teaching." In *Shakespeare in the Changing Curriculum,* edited by L. Aers and N. Wheale, 40–57. London: Routledge.

Barnhouse, R. 1998. "Books and Reading in Young Adult Literature Set in the Middle Ages." *The Lion and the Unicorn.* 22: 364–375.

——— *Recasting the Past: The Middle Ages in Young Adult Literature.* 2000. Portsmouth, New Hampshire: Heinemann–Boynton/Cook.

Bottoms, J. 1996. "Of *Tales* and *Tempests.*" *Children's Literature in Education.* 27 (2): 73–86.

Carroll, W. C. (1999). *Macbeth: Texts and Contexts,* by W. Shakespeare. Boston: Bedford/St. Martin's.

Gurr, A. 1992. *The Shakespearean Stage 1574–1642.* 3rd ed. Cambridge: Cambridge University Press.

Hanawalt, B. 1993. *Growing Up in Medieval London: The Experience of Childhood in History.* New York: Oxford University Press.

Herz, S. K. and D. R. Gallo. 1996. *From Hinton to Hamlet: Building Bridges Between Young Adult Literature and the Classics*. Westport, Connecticut: Greenwood Press.

Hunt, P. 1997. "Afterword," *In the Best of Shakespeare: Retellings of 10 Classic Plays*, by E. Nesbit, 103–08. Oxford: Oxford University Press.

Jardine, L. 1996. *Reading Shakespeare Historically*. London: Routledge.

McDonald, R. 1996. *The Bedford Companion to Shakespeare: An Introduction with Documents*. New York: St. Martin's Press.

O'Brien. P., Ed. 1993–1995. *Shakespeare Set Free*. 3 vols. New York: Washington Square Press.

Orgel, S., Ed. 1994 (1987). *The Tempest*. New York: Oxford University Press.

Pollock, L. 1983. *Forgotten Children: Parent–Child Relations from 1500–1900*. Cambridge: Cambridge University Press.

Reed, A. J. S. 1993. "Using Young Adult Literature to Modernize the Teaching of *Romeo and Juliet*." In *Adolescent Literature as a Complement to the Classics*, edited by Joan F. Kaywell, 93–115. Norwood, MA: Christopher-Gordon Publishers, Inc.

Shapiro, J. 1996. *Shakespeare and the Jews*. New York: Columbia University Press.

Sommerville, C.J. 1992. *The Discovery of Childhood in Puritan England*. Athens: University of Georgia Press.

Stephens, J. 1997. "Not Unadjacent to a Play About a Scottish King: Terry Pratchett Retells *Macbeth*." *Papers: Explorations into Children's Literature*. 7 (2): 29–37.

Stewig, J. W. 1995. "The Witch Woman: A Recurring Motif in Recent Fantasy Writing for Young Readers." *Children's Literature in Education*. 26 (2): 119–133.

Stone, L. 1977. *The Family, Sex, and Marriage in England 1500–1800*. New York: Harper & Row.

Taylor, G. 1989. *Reinventing Shakespeare: A Cultural History from the Restoration to the Present*. New York: Winfield and Nicolson.

Thompson A. and S. Roberts, eds. 1997. *Women Reading Shakspeare, 1660–1900: An Anthology of Criticism*. New York: Manchester University Press.

Wrightson, K. 1982. *English Society 1580–1680*. Rutgers, New York: Rutgers University Press.

Index